Andrew,
God bless the Order
of the Tobacconst!
Zach Bartels

"I intend to smoke a good cigar to the glory of God before I go to bed to-night.

–Rev. Charles H. Spurgeon

September 20, 1874

The Christian Gentleman's
Smoking Companion

Ted Kluck
&
Zach Bartels

www.gutcheckpress.com

The Christian Gentleman's Smoking Companion

Published by Gut Check Press—Lansing, Michigan

Requests for information may be directed through http://www.gutcheckpress.com

ISBN 978-0-9830783-5-7

Photographs © 2013 by Erin Bartels

Published in association with K-D Enterprises.

For Tim Socier

Friend, Spiritual Mentor,
Tobacconist

INTRODUCTION: WHY A CHRISTIAN SMOKING COMPANION?

If you're a loyal and dedicated fan of Gut Check Press, perhaps you've been astonished by the rich characters and tight storyline in our DispenSensational™ end-times thriller, have laughed at or been massively offended by our Post-modern and Reformed satires, or eagerly anticipate reading our children's book[1] around the hearth with your eleven Reformed children. Perhaps you've also asked yourself, "Why have these accomplished men—artists, moguls—never endeavored to write the comprehensive guide-to-slash-celebration-of cigar smoking for the Christian man?" An honest question, to be sure.

Maybe it's because we've been busy writing other books (me, and Zach), pastoring a church (Zach), molding young minds in the classroom (me), and making—wait for it—one point eight *thousand* dollars (Gut Check Corporate). Nevertheless, the cigar book is here and we can all rest a little easier. I was once asked in a Big Media Interview, when I thought my career would be complete. I stroked my painstakingly stubbled beard, removed my obviously-aff-ected hipster glasses, and rubbed my temples before replying, "When Gut Check Press releases the comprehen-sive guide-to-slash-celebration-of cigar smoking for the Christian man." The statement was met with stunned, reverent, impressed silence.[2]

Zach and I are Christians and we love cigars. We're both appreciators of history and, as such, we love the simplicity and aesthetic of the cigar, whose design and production hasn't changed much in, oh, forever. On a recent trip to Miami, I had the opportunity to speak at a church cigar event (more on this later) and visit a cigar factory, and it's as though I was transported back in time. The cigar is a sensory experience, and the factory was filled with the rich sights and smells that I love.

I have confessed sin over cigars, asked for prayer over cigars, celebrated personal and professional victories over cigars, and mourned personal and professional defeats over cigars. I've laughed with those who have laughed, over cigars, and wept with those who have wept.

That's not to elevate the cigar to some kind of exalted religious or cultural level. Here's what a cigar is, in plain-speak: An excuse to sit down and talk with another guy for an hour. Think about it . . . when does this *ever* happen outside a cigar lounge? When guys are "hunting together" they're sitting in a tree stand being quiet. When guys are "watching a ballgame together" they're sitting in a living room or a sports bar staring slack-jawed at a television. When guys are "shopping for antiques together"[3] they're walking through a junky antique store making fun of all the ridiculous stuff inside and not really talking about the stuff of life.

The cigar lounge removes the awkward stiltedness of the Church Lobby ("How are YOU doing Bob?"), and it's not as formal and intimidating as a counselor's office, yet it still works as a place to talk.

That is to say, the cigar has played an important role in our spiritual and social lives and chances are, if you've picked up this book, you feel the same way. Inside we'll talk some cigar-selecting basics, discuss what to look for in a cigar lounge, spin out a few self-indulgent narratives, crack large amounts of wise, and share true wisdom from some great cigar-loving theologians, past and present.

This book is intended to occupy a prominent place on your coffee table and in your heart.

Enjoy.

Ted Kluck
Co-Founder, Secretary of the Interior
Gut Check Press

Are Cigars and Pipes Sinful?

You may have picked up this book for a good leafing-through because the very idea seemed bizarre to you. After all, isn't the very notion of smoking *worldly*? If you're asking this question, this book is not for you. Not because you're less sophisticated than us or "don't get it" or anything like that, but because we do not want you to violate your conscience in any way. We take very seriously the warnings in Romans 14 and I Corinthians 8-10 about creating stumbling blocks and doing damage to a brother or sister's faith.

But here's the thing: we have to trust you to hear us on this and put the book down, because the problem with all the technology that brought this volume from our heads to your hands (from Amazon.com and its cousins to digital printing and computer-coordinated, decentralized shipping) is that such a universal reach takes the nuance out of the kind of case-by-case appraisal St. Paul modeled and commanded.

The fact is that there are many areas of the English-speaking world where there is truly no connection whatsoever (and never has been) between enjoying a pipe or cigar and *worldliness*, even in theologically conservative settings. There are also very solid Christian traditions in which, regardless of geography, a pint of beer or a fine cigar is considered a great gift from the Maker of All Good Things without any undesirable baggage. (Confessional Lutherans, I'm looking at you . . .)

Let me take off my Gut Check Mogul Helmet for a minute and put on my Theologian Cap (it looks like the one John Calvin's wearing in all the pictures). Pipes and cigars fall into the broad category of what we would call *adiaphora*—that which is neither mandated nor clearly prohibited in Scripture. St. Paul calls these "disputable matters" (Rom 14:1). In these gray areas (e.g. the eating of certain meats; see I Cor 8, Rom 14), we want to avoid either of two extremes:

1. An ascetic, legalistic stance (i.e., "Touch not, taste not, handle not," Col 2:21), which implies that food can only be

eaten for sustenance, rather than pleasure, and sex must be reserved for procreation, never enjoyed as a good gift from God. If we embraced this view, we would further conclude that, since cigars serve no non-aesthetic purpose (unless you ask Spurgeon, see page 31), they should be avoided altogether. However, the New Testament frequently *refutes* such a view (e.g., Col 2:20, Matt 15:11).

2. The opposite error is an antinomian, self-centered approach to liberty, in which we throw off restraint and become obsessed with our own "rights" and enjoyment of this life as if we were supposed to live our best life *now*—effectively trying to become "Christian hedonists," but not in the way John Piper meant when he coined the term.

Speaking of Piper, he recognizes the tension here, in that he counts the habitual inhaling of cigarette smoke as sinful (a habit he feels communicates the philosophy, "Life doesn't matter as much as my pleasures do"),[4] but labels "hang-ups with smoking" as a "pietistic, perfectionist tendency"[5] and counts that category as one of Fundamentalism's shortcomings.

Tim Challies cites the above Piper quotes in his very thoughtful article "Is Smoking Sinful?" which explores "both sides" of this discussion and comes to a balanced conclusion.[6] The reason this gets tricky is because these issues resist the simple list of "do's and don'ts" we crave in the flesh, requiring us to embrace the tension between Christian liberty and our brother's conscience, while giving deference to the latter.

A word of caution: while I have no real beef with the KJV (hey, if it was good enough for John the Baptist . . .), beware of selective anachronistic appeal to verses about "offending" your brother, which are often played liberally as trump cards. In 1611, the word "offendeth" adequately conveyed the idea of a stumbling block. Today, though, mature Christians can easily be *offended* (modern definition) by the presence of your cigar smoke or the fact that you indulge such a "stinky practice," without being in any danger of falling into sin because of it, and having no "former associations" (I Cor 8:7) between sin and smoke. The New Testament has no instructions for us regarding this "annoyed brother," and so common courtesy must make up the difference.

At the end of the day, though, while we may love a fine cigar on a summer evening and while we are free in Christ to enjoy one—indeed *because* we so enjoy a fine cigar and are free to do so—the real question is: are we willing to set aside that freedom in any setting where exercising it might cause a brother or sister to stumble? Are we willing to show that kind of "servant of all" mentality, even if it means giving up one of our rights? I would suggest that, in regards to disputable matters, remaining "above reproach" does not mean denying oneself everything from caffeinated beverages to shellfish to target shooting to Twister to pipe tobacco to TV game shows like some sort of Pharisee-on-steroids, as if to anticipate everyone's hang-ups and avoid them entirely. Rather, it means being willing—entirely willing—to lay aside our freedoms to avoid shipwrecking our brother's faith.

We encourage you to use both courtesy and discernment in this matter, remembering that, with *adiaphora* one must take into account not only geographic, but temporal differences. There was a time in this land when most Christians would never be seen at a "movie house" (not even to see a wholesome film) or play with the "devil's cards" (not even bridge or euchre) or attend a child's magic show(!)[7] because these things had a stigma and it was assumed that taking part in them would hurt the Church's witness.[8] These stigma have, by and large, passed away in the majority of communities, and might I suggest that the pipe and cigar have become similarly mainstream and de-stigmatized (even while smoking in public has become less permitted) such that, unless there is particular reason for caution (i.e. new converts present, someone with a past of addiction and partying, etc.), we may, like Spurgeon, smoke a cigar to the glory of God!

Zach Bartels
Co-Founder, Key Grip, Chaplain
Gut Check Press

STEVE BROWN

Dr. Steve Brown is and has been many things, including a pastor, seminary professor, author, and radio personality. Through his Key Life Network and ever-edgy radio program *Steve Brown, etc.*, Dr. Brown has a way of simultaneously getting under your skin and opening your eyes to the Truth of God's Word. He also loves smoking his pipe, which itself has become an emblem of Christian liberty and conversation-starter re: practical holiness.

"After a dull sermon, a boring faculty meeting, a hard day, etc., one needs something to look forward to. In that way, smoking is like heaven. It, of course, isn't heaven, but it will do until then."

—Steve Brown

WHAT TO LOOK FOR IN A CIGAR LOUNGE: IN PRAISE OF TIMOTHY'S FINE CIGARS

Bay City, Michigan, is a lot like other Midwestern, mid-sized cities. Downtown is a little hip (there's a 1920s gangster-themed restaurant and a soon-to-be out-of-business "international café" where you can get an overpriced veggie wrap[9]), a little old-fashioned (a strip of antique stores that I'm ashamed to say I frequent), and currently in the midst of some urban renewal (i.e., the mountains of gravel along the river are being replaced with overpriced condos).

What differentiates Bay City from those other cities is that it contains what I believe to be the Midwest's premiere cigar lounge, Timothy's Fine Cigars. What, you ask, makes a good cigar lounge? Ahh, the criteria are probably as varied and unique and numerous as cigar smokers themselves. Here are a few:

1. An Aesthetic that is Decidedly Masculine But Isn't In Any Way Dirty or Seedy

Zach and I used to favor some other cigar lounges, closer to home (Timothy's is an hour drive away), which at any given time were populated by a self-styled soldier of fortune who has probably killed people with his bare hands (we set the number at 3-5 people killed, est.), a formerly-successful Big Time Lawyer who now swills vodka out of an empty Wendy's cup, and a gigantic, dirty man with a huge beard, who you can hear sort of wheezing in and out. Out of the corner of one particular lounge blares a gigantic television (cool) with a non-stop feed of depressing news stories (not cool). In the back of said lounge is probably the dirtiest bathroom on earth, and I die a little bit inside each time I have to use it, which isn't very often.

By contrast, Timothy's is well-lit, and decorated with a wide array of tobacco memorabilia—everything from antique advertisements to banners and posters from current vendors. There's a circular array of fine leather chairs that invites dialogue from other patrons, but doesn't demand it.

2. A Proprietor Who Makes You Feel Sufficiently Tough But Doesn't Make You Feel Like You Might Get Shot

One of the sublime pleasures of the cigar store is the sense that it's a little "underground," a little "private," and a little "off limits." That is to say, you can go there and not have to worry about running into that chatty couple from the Soccer Boosters Club at your kids' school. Still, if the place is a little *too* seedy—i.e., if the proprietor seems to be either a.) drunk or b.) doing something illegal all the time—it can seriously hinder your enjoyment.

Tim walks this line well. He always has a good story to tell and/or a good movie recommendation, but he also gives the sense that he's a competent, successful businessman who knows what he's doing and runs a safe, clean, above-board establishment.

3. A Proprietor Who Knows When To Stop Talking and Just Let You Enjoy the Cigar

This one is self-explanatory.

4. A Clean Bathroom

There are several things I love about the bathroom at Timothy's. First and foremost, it's clean. Yeah, I'm a masculine tough-guy and all that, but I still don't want to feel like I need to stop by the doctor's office for some pen-

Your chosen cigar lounge should make you feel like you're the money.

icillin and antibiotic salve after using certain bathrooms. Two, there are framed, autographed advertisements on the walls from some of the cigar industry's greatest families. Three, there's a urinal. Four, there's a little ledge above the urinal upon which sits a convenient single-cigar ashtray. Five, it smells like lilacs.

Quick story about the bathroom at Timothy's: I was on my way out of the bathroom once, when another patron tried the door, found it locked, and swore loudly. Seconds later, I opened the door and he said, sheepishly, "Oh good, I was just about to curse you," to which I replied, "You did curse me. I heard you." To which he said nothing and just looked at me sheepishly.

5. A Cigars-Only Vibe

Traditional pipes are okay as well, of course, but if the cigar place in question also sells any of the following: bongs, rolling papers, cheap off-brand cigarettes—you're no longer in a cigar lounge but have somehow stumbled into a "discount tobacco place that just happens to carry cigars." Leave immediately.

6. Good Cigars

This one is also self-explanatory, and you might think it would be a "given" for most cigar lounges, but it isn't. Timothy's has a great array of cigars, from affordable entry-level smokes to the kinds of special occasion-level cigars you only spring for when you've just gotten married, conquered your industry, or annexed a small country. A good proprietor will show you around the humidor, but will leave you alone to make a selection, and won't judge the selection you do make.

7. Other Clientele Who Don't Make You Feel Depressed

I'm an introvert, so my idea of good Other Clientele is the clientele who just aren't there. An empty cigar lounge is the best cigar lounge. However, here are some archetypes to avoid:

- *The React Loudly to Televised Sports Guy.* This guy wants you to know that he's watching the ballgame, and does so by reacting loudly to it and inviting you to comment.

- *The Networker.* This guy has something he wants to buy, sell, or process, and he wants to share this unique opportunity with you.

- *The Fake Author.* This one is germane to us because we're authors and we run a publishing imprint, but the Fake Author wants you to know that he's "written and published" books of his own.[10] If there's anyone else in the cigar lounge, odds are—oh, let's say 100% that there is a fake author present.

- *The Drunk Guy Who's Just Looking for a Place to Sit Down.* Self-explanatory.

- *The Guffawing With His Friends Guy.* This guy hardly ever goes to a cigar lounge, but he's here today with his "buddies" to have some loud, obnoxious "guy time!" Avoid.

WHAT YOUR FACE LOOKS LIKE IF YOU SUBSIST ON CIGARS AND SCOTCH: IN PRAISE OF JAMES SUCKLING

Who, you might ask, is James Suckling and why are we praising him? James Suckling is the editor-in-chief *of Cigar Aficionado* magazine, which you may know better as the "magazine for people who can afford a $95,000 car and who have a private yacht." Still, we love *Cigar Aficionado* because it's where you can read mostly-meaningless reviews with phrases like, "this cigar has a nice draw, but a woody, flinty finish with hints of oil."

There are two great things about James Suckling. One, his name. Often performers like Rock Stars will affect a stage name like Jo-Jo Rocket or Johnny Bravo[11] or Madonna. Either Suckling was born with the perfect name for a cigar critic, or he affected it in the fashion of the aforementioned Rock Stars. Either way, it's absolutely perfect.

The other great thing about James Suckling is his face, which always accompanies his column in the magazine. Suckling's face perfectly matches his name, inasmuch as it looks like he has been "suckling" cigars since early childhood. I can imagine young Suckling sitting around shooting marbles with his peers at Taft Elementary, hustling them out of their hard-earned pennies, while chewing the end of a crude, depression-era cigar. I can imagine a slightly-older Suckling in college, bedecked in a dapper suit of clothes, with a fine looking young lady on his arm, puffing a cigar that he bought by trading in all of his textbooks and then seducing all of his professors in order to pass his courses. When you're James Suckling, this is what you do.[12]

Then you sit around with all your friends and guffaw about it. Suckling's present-day face is a study in what happens to the human face if that human does nothing but drink high-end scotch and smoke hand-made cigars. His skin has actually begun to take on the patina of a Connecticut-shade cigar wrapper. His eyes are deep-set in dark, cavernous circles, as though if you were to cut open James Suckling's face it would be like that scene in *National Lampoon's Christmas Vacation* where Clark Griswold cuts open the dry turkey and a bunch of smoke billows out.

Of course, I've never met James Suckling, so I don't know if any of this is true. If I ever were to meet Suckling, it would either be a.) in an exclusive, members-only casino in Rio De Janiero; b.) on the tarmac of an undisclosed airport whilst gassing up our private jets; or c.) at Timothy's Fine Cigars in Bay City, Michigan.

So here's to you, Jim. Shine on, you suckling diamond.

To Kill a Mockingbird

Atticus "Suckling" Finch: "Miss Ewell did something that in our society was unspeakable—she ate a chicken dish and paired it with a simple red table wine. Thomas Jefferson once said that 'all men are created equal.' But we know for a fact that some people are smarter than others, some are more gifted than others, and some smoke better cigars than others. I am one of those people. I rest my case."

Noah (from the Bible)

In the biblical account of Noah, a man is chosen by God to construct an ark, which will save two of each of earth's animals, as well as Noah's family. Instead, Noah (Suckling), decides to re-appropriate some of the rich mahogany[13] in order to craft a giant, floating ark to house and protect his significant selection of cigars and smoking accessories. In addition to the expansive wine cellar which takes up the bottom third of the ark, Noah decides, in the interest of taste, to only invite animals on board that contribute to an "upscale aesthetic," and when he realizes that this eliminates all animals except certain varieties of tropical fish (duh, it's a flood), he decides instead to just bring lots of cognac, used books, and a few girls he met while on a cigar tasting expedition in Europe.

Twilight

Rather than being a vampire who drinks blood, Edward Suckling is a middle-aged aesthete who has an affinity for rich Cab/Savs and strong maduros. Because of this, he is noncommittal toward the film's other lead character, Bella Swan, who is a teenager (creepy?) and who, Suckling thinks, is a little pale and for whom a little sunlight would do some good. Swan thinks Suckling's obsession with wine and cigars is "boring" (her words) and is as a result drawn headlong into a relationship with the character who regularly turns into a wolf. She is eventually eaten (because she's in love with a wolf) while Suckling is away on a golf trip and the entire series suffers as a result.

Amadeus

Antonio "Suckling" Salieri, while reflecting on how to kill Amadeus: "The only thing that worried me was the actual killing. How does one do that? How does one kill a man? It's one thing to dream about it . . . very different when you have to do it with your own hands—hands that are filled with a cup of fine, warming cognac and an Ashton Maduro."

Say Anything

Lloyd "Suckling" Dobler, upon meeting Diane Cort's overbearing father James for the first time at a dinner party and being asked what he wants to do for a living, says, "I don't want to buy anything, sell anything, or process anything . . . I actually want to be an upscale aesthete, traveling the world in search of the perfect wine and cigar pairings and then writing about them in various niche publications. I also want to be a kickboxer."

DIETRICH BONHOEFFER

Bonhoeffer is famous for his incredible work *The Cost of Discipleship*, for his pivotal role in founding the German Confessing Church, and for being affiliated with an anti-Nazi group that tried on multiple occasions to assassinate Hitler (who was, incidentally, stridently anti-smoking). Bonhoeffer greatly enjoyed smoking cigars, pipes, and cigarettes. His collected letters from the last year and a half of his life contain many a reference to smoking materials (see below), which were at least as much a comfort to him as books of poetry, writing paper, ink, and shaving cream. Apparently, even in a Nazi-controlled prison, the act of smoking calmed him and helped him to focus on God.

"The cigars [you sent] are most magnificent . . . I am very grateful for any smoking supplies."

-Dietrich Bonhoeffer

THE COMPONENTS OF A CIGAR

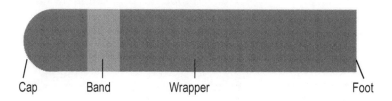

| Cap | Band | Wrapper | Foot |

Cigars are more complex than most people assume and creating high-quality cigars is a skill that requires many years to master. Premium brands have more experienced / talented rollers than lesser labels, which is every bit as important as using quality tobacco. Fine cigar companies will limit the number rolled per day, rather than maximize, in order to ensure quality and protect their brand's reputation, taking redundant precautions to make sure that every cigar that receives a band deserves one. Yes, this is tantamount to becoming an expert in any highly skilled field. And yet, the whole thing is simple enough that anyone can appreciate how they're made and what goes into them:

Sun-Grown Plant

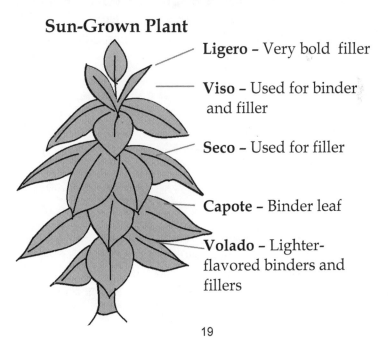

Ligero – Very bold filler

Viso – Used for binder and filler

Seco – Used for filler

Capote – Binder leaf

Volado – Lighter-flavored binders and fillers

Filler

Before we look at the filler, realize that, not only are there many different breeds of the tobacco plant and many different methods of harvesting and preparing, which make for very different kinds of smoking experiences, but that the various parts of each tobacco plant are each used for a different part of the cigar (not unlike the noble Native American wasting no part of the buffalo).

Ligero (i.e. top leaves, seeing the most direct sunlight and having the most intense flavor) are used for filler, as are the subtler **seco** and **volado** (which are lowest on the plant). Filler is the tobacco inside the cigar, supplying the majority of the flavor. The tobacco in a fine cigar is comprised of a **blend** of up to four different distinct fillers. The way a cigar's filler is prepared dictates, in a sense, the first classification of what kind of cigar we're dealing with. We can break it down into three groups:

- LONG FILL: Intact leaves that run long-ways down the cigar (i.e. the filler is *long*, hence "long fill"), indicating a higher quality blend and delivering a much better tasting, more uniform, more enjoyable experience.

- SHORT FILL: Scraps, trimmings, and leaf hash held in place by the wrapper (such cigars generally do not have a binder leaf—see below). This is generally what you will find in lower-quality and machine-made cigars. If this is all new information to you, you might be thinking, "Hey, it's all going to burn up anyway; who cares if the tobacco starts out chopped up or long and intact?"

Let me use an analogy from the world of horrible fried foods here. Have you ever eaten *real* onion rings from a mom and pop restaurant or diner? They come in infinite different sizes and shapes because an *actual* ring of the onion was dipped in batter and tossed in the fryer. Now, have you ever had fast food onion rings? I know, right? You know why they suck? Because they're comprised of minced onion refuse mixed into some non-nutritive clear food gel (probably designed by the aforementioned Clark W. Griswald), and machine dipped in some feeble excuse for batter. That's the difference (oh, I hate myself for saying this) between a long-fill and a short-fill cigar. Besides, you saw the word "scraps," right? These scraps simply don't taste good, which is why all kinds of chemicals and fruity flavors are often added to cover up the natural taste of the tobacco.

- MIXED FILL: A combination of long and short-filler, found in mid-level cigars.

Binder Leaf

Have you ever smoked a dried-out cigar and had the outside unravel and come right off?[14] You finished it anyway—didn't you?—because you're Dutch and because it was still basically a cigar, just not as pretty. The reason it held its shape is because of the binder leaf (**capote**), which is basically the *dermis* of the smoke. It holds the filler in place and maintains the *ring gauge*. Binders are sometimes made of **volado** or **viso** (see diagram, p. 19). If an otherwise wrapper-worthy leaf is discolored, punctured, or has too prominent of veins, the leaf may be relegated to binder duty.

Wrapper

In general, tobacco plants grown in the sun are used for binders and fillers, while shade-grown plants are used for the wrappers. This is the cigar's *epidermis*, the outer skin, which needs to communicate to the prospective smoker what lies within. The color and feel of the wrapper tells a story—and it *contributes* to the story as well. A good wrapper puts the finish on a fine cigar's flavor, which is why that dry, wrapperless cigar you went ahead and finished didn't just make you look stupid; it didn't taste right either.

Hand-Made vs. Hand-Rolled

At this point, you should be able to quickly spot the difference between mass-produced, machine-made factory junk and fine, hand-made cigars. A true cigar-lover will always opt for fewer of the latter over many of the former.

However, it gets a little confusing when we introduce the distinction between "hand-made" and "hand-rolled." Here's the skinny: **hand-made** cigars were made by hand (duh) with simple tools and no mechanical or factory intrusion. The term **hand-rolled** on the other . . . um . . . *hand* refers to a cigar whose filler was bunched by machine and then had the wrapper applied by hand by a cigar roller. These often contain short filler. (A good indicator or whether a cigar contains long or short filler is the length of the ash; if you achieve a long ash, you're definitely not smoking a short-fill.)

Suggested Display Options

Let's just break from the cigar lessons for a moment to talk logistics. Being that this is a coffee table book, of sorts, it is imperative that you display it on a coffee table. That may sound obvious, but we've been moguls in the book business long enough to know that sometimes you need to tell people how to display the book you've just sold them. Sometimes you actually need to tell them how to feel about the book you've just sold them but, alas, that's another essay for another time (read: probably later in this book).

But seriously. Let's just state the obvious (because it's the elephant in the room): this book is a little *small* to merit consideration next to expensive, glossy, pictorial coffee-table books like the book you probably own with all the depressing pictures of post-apocalyptic Detroit and also the book on Michigan Lighthouses. Those are fine books. What I'm saying is, go ahead and proudly display this book right alongside (or even instead-of).

What you're pre-supposing is that the coffee table itself is a certain size. What I'm pre-supposing is, "What if it isn't?" Like people, coffee tables come in all shapes and sizes. And we appreciate and celebrate coffee tables of all shapes and sizes. Like, perhaps your mom has one of those small,

end-of-the-sofa coffee tables (nay, "end tables"). This would go great on one of those.

There's also the coffee table that your wife picked up off the side of the road and then mosaic-tiled over back when people were doing that. There's also the $1,000 Pottery Barn coffee table fashioned in the style of a rusted farm implement. There's also the coffee table that sits so low to the ground that it appears that people should be kneeling, having a Karate-Kid-II-style tea service at it, like the one that took place between Kumiko and Daniel-san. If you're a hipster, perhaps you've fashioned a coffee table out of an old tubular television or you threw an old, distressed door up on some saw-horses.

Our book would look great on any of those coffee tables.

Maybe you're not the coffee table type. It's okay. We celebrate you too. May we suggest a glass case with a rotating turntable underneath it? Maybe a dedicated book stand, like the one on which you would put an antique Bible. You may even put it on a bookshelf, but I suggest turning the cover out (known to us, in the business, as "facing" it). Perhaps you could even put it on a sad folding table in the narthex of your church (i.e., "Book Table") and sell copies of it.

RALPH ERSKINE

As a Calvinist clergyman, I'm often annoyed at the way Puritans are portrayed in our culture as pleasure-haters and kill-joys. Historically, Puritans have been neither. They loved good food and good alcohol (in moderation), and celebrated good sex. While they were split about tobacco smoking (some associated it with idleness), at least one great Puritan—the Scottish churchman Ralph Erskine—was smitten enough with the idea of pipe-smoking to write the following poem about it, using tobacco in a series of metaphors to illustrate the Gospel and Christian devotion.

Smoking Spiritualized. In Two Parts, by Ralph Erskine

Part I

This Indian weed now wither´d quite,
Though green at noon, cut down at night,
Shows thy decay;
All flesh is hay.
Thus think, and smoke tobacco.

The pipe so lily-like and weak,
Does thus thy mortal state bespeak.
Thou are ev´n such,
Gone with a touch.
Thus think, and smoke tobacco.

All when the smoke ascends on high,
Then thou behold´st the vanity
Of worldly stuff,
Gone with a puff.
Thus think, and smoke tobacco.

And when the pipe grows foul within,
Think on thy soul defil´d with sin;
For then the fire,
It does require.
Thus think, and smoke tobacco.

And seest the ashes cast away;
Then to thyself thou mayest say,
That to the dust
Return thou must.
Thus think, and smoke tobacco.

Part II

Was this small plant for thee cut down?
So was the Plant of great renown;
Which mercy sends
For nobler ends.
Thus think, and smoke tobacco.

Doth juice medicinal proceed
From such a naughty foreign weed?
Then what´s the pow´r
Of Jesse´s flow´r?
Thus think, and smoke tobacco.

The promise, like the pipe inlays,
And by the mouth of faith conveys
What virtue flows
From Sharon´s rose.
Thus think, and smoke tobacco.

In vain the´unlighted pipe you blow;
Your pains in outward means are so,
Till heav´nly fire
The heart inspire.
Thus think, and smoke tobacco.

The smoke, like burning incense, tow´rs;
So should a praying heart of yours,
With ardent cries,
Surmont the skies.
Thus think, and smoke tobacco.

Shades of Wrappers

As we mentioned, the wrapper of a fine cigar should let you know what is in store for you should you smoke it. Occasionally you'll find a smoke whose wrapper clashes with the filler. Put these on a list of cigars in your mind that are "dead to you." Most of the time, though, the wrapper doesn't lie. As with coffee, the darker the wrapper, the stronger the body (with some rare exceptions).

Since this isn't a full-color book, we're going to need you to use your imagination here, as we go from lightest to darkest.[15]

DOUBLE CLARO (sometimes called a Candela): This is a greenish tan wrapper. These cigars have been harvested early and dried in an accelerated process (often by applying much heat), rather than being air-cured like God intended. Garcia y Vega is an example of these. Avoid.

CLARO These can be divided into two subcategories: Natural Claro (very light) and Colorado Claro (a little darker). This shade is achieved by intentionally harvesting early, but properly drying the leaves, producing a nice, mild smoke.

COLORADO This is the color cigars are in the mind of a non-smoker: a middlish tan/brown, either with or without a touch of red.

MADURO: Dark brown. These are very strong. When they're good (e.g. one of my favorite cigars, the Montecristo Reserva Negra), they're *very* good. When they're bad, they're boldly bad. Ashton makes some solid-but-affordable maduros.

DOUBLE MADURO Also sometimes called "oscuro," this is kind of a . . . um . . . burnt umber? Is that a color? It's really, really dark brown—the result of a very late harvest and being aged longer before being rolled.

If you've been randomly selecting cigars from all over the continuum, you may want to work your way from the lighter stuff to the darker. Also note, some very skilled cigar rollers will create a "barber pole" effect by combining two different wrappers. When done well, this can be a very nuanced smoke.

I'M WITH RUIZ: EL LECTOR, CIGARS, AND CHURCH

Miami is a unique town. It's fun, but I wouldn't call it relaxing. It's a cultural foil to the Midwest in every way—it's flashy, confusing, multicultural, and warm (meteorologically, if not interpersonally). It's in that environment that Granada Presbyterian Church thrives and teaches a gospel of God's grace to men and women. One of Granada's ministries is a men's outreach called "El Lector" which is patterned after the old tradition of having an author read to 19th century Cuban cigar rollers while they work (pause now to appreciate how utterly cool this is.)

Granada member, entrepreneur, and Renaissance man Marcos Ruiz launched the event, which has played host to authors, filmmakers, actors, and cigar families. Ruiz hatched the idea because he felt a lack of non-awkward, non-forced-feeling church events for men. He wanted something that wasn't another golf league (meh) and wasn't another wee-hours-of-the-morning men's Bible study. He wanted a place to smoke a cigar with other Christians and with men who were curious about the Gospel.

The event has thrived and is itself an extension of a cigar/discussion group called "Eagle and Child Forum" (named after the pub where Lewis and Tolkein used to hang out) which was launched by Ruiz and informally covers everything from literature to tobacco to Scripture. In short, Ruiz is the guy you wish you had at your church because he's cool to hang out with and has the rocks to try to pull something like this off. Before the event he bought me breakfast at a Cuban diner, toured me around a cigar factory, and showed me a Coral Gables hotel where Al Capone used to crash.

Hosted in the Granada Pres courtyard (think: palm trees, warm breeze, stucco), El Lector included great food (wings, fried mushrooms, lots of cheese), drink, and premium cigars from the Torano Cigar Family—attended to by an exceedingly cool guy named Jack Torano who told me stories about the following (among others): Aaron "The Hawk" Pryor, the lead singer of "Survivor," how his family got into the cigar business, and the Bud Light "Real Men of Genius" ad campaign which he helped record. He absolutely should have been the speaker.

But I was the speaker, and I had an amazing time. I spoke about two of my favorite things: boxing and the glorious grace of the Gospel of Jesus Christ. In the audience were Granada Pres members, their friends, and random guys from around the city of Miami who had seen the ad, and who were interested in hearing me talk about a Mike Tyson boxing book I once wrote.

So is a cigar outreach like this right for every church? Of course not. There are places where something like that would still freak everyone out and may divisively do more harm than good. Miami is not one of those places. Miami is a place where the cigar is a part of the local culture, and thus the idea of a cigar at a church event isn't a big deal for people. But considering an El Lector-ish event in your church or area *might* be the right thing to do. It will almost certainly be a lot of fun to plan and execute. If you're interested, hit up Marcos through one of the links below, and I'm sure he'll be glad to give you pointers on how to plan the event and how to partner with a local cigar proprietor in your area.

The point of El Lector is to provide a place where a man—perhaps an unchurched man, even—feels comfortable, so that he can later feel uncomfortable (because of his sin), and then later be introduced to the God of all comfort, our Lord Jesus Christ. In that paradigm, the cigar seems pretty inconsequential (and it is), however, it is the thing around which we all, initially, gather.

For more info on Granada Pres, visit: http://granadapca.org

For more info on El Lector, visit:
www.facebook.com/ellectorspeakerseries

To buy a few boxes of Torano Cigars, visit: www.torano.com

C.H. SPURGEON

Charles Haddon Spurgeon has been a controversial, yet universally-loved institution since he began preaching in his youth. He is known by many titles, including the Prince of Preachers, the Duke of Awesomeness, and the Protestant Patron Saint of Puffing. Yes, we suppose it's ironic that a Baptist preacher is the most well-known cigar smoker in Christian history, seeing as how Baptist preachers stereotypically eschew all creeds except "We don't smoke, we don't chew, we don't go with girls who do" [16] But Spurgeon, who was mastered by nothing save Christ, understood what a good cigar could do, when properly enjoyed.

"When I have found intense pain relieved, a weary brain soothed, and calm refreshing sleep obtained by a cigar, I have felt grateful to God and have blessed his name."

-Rev. Charles H. Spurgeon

BODY AND FLAVOR

When talking about the experience of smoking a cigar, there are two basic categories (although any number of supplementals could be added):

Body: Body is distinct from "flavor" and is generally limited to designating a light, medium, or full strength cigar. Some cigars that have almost no taste are very *strong* all the same (and therefore have body). Strong cigars often leave your mouth feeling "walked through" the next morning, regardless of how much mouthwash you've used (although this is less the case with very high-end smokes).

Flavor: This is a far more subjective category and your imagination and pretentiousness are the only limits on how you can describe it. Just be sure to use words you'd never use in real life so you sound sophisticated and worldly. Actually, scratch that; as a Christian (especially a cigar-smoking Christian), the last thing you want is to sound worldly.[17]

You've probably seen the reviews in high-end smoking magazines that read like some kind of example from the deeper end of the DSM-IV: "This cigar featured hints of fresh nineteenth-century Parisian croissants mixed with all-spice and aged leather basketball, with a slight oak-chrysanthemum finish." Don't try to sound like these guys. To do so is an offense on par with announcing, "Looks like some-body's got a case of the *Mondays!*" Oh, and why does one of these guys always have to be tasting chocolate in these reviews? If I tasted *chocolate* (either "hints" or "overtones" or whatever) in a cigar, I'd demand my money back.

My favorite way to describe flavor is with words like "delicious" or "awful," but you should run with whatever works for you. More importantly, try to develop a taste for a wide range of cigars, recognizing that you will not want the same type of smoke with a golf foursome at 9 AM as you would with an afternoon coffee or an after-dinner cigar with brandy.

About Those Cubans. . .

Whenever the topic of cigars comes up in the presence of non-smokers, you can probably safely hold your breath until someone raises the topic of Cuban cigars. "Have you ever had a Cuban?" someone might ask, a gleam in his eye, as he has (he thinks) smoked a genuine—*gasp!*—Cuban cigar! Or maybe he knows a guy who has a connection to someone who illegally (read: allegedly) imports Cubans through Manitoba.

Because of Cuba's history as a cigar powerhouse and the current "forbidden fruit" aspect caused by the trade embargo, Cuban cigars are assumed by the general populace (and backed up by television) to be the ultimate indulgence for a cigar smoker.

But here's the truth: if someone offers you a Cuban cigar or claims to have smoked a Cuban whilst overseas on vacation, the cigars in question were more than likely bought at a resort or from a street vendor. And they're usually about as Cuban as that Subway sandwich with the pulled pork and pickles. A healthy skepticism is always in order in such situations.

And even if you can confirm geographic origin, a recently-made Cuban cigar is not necessarily the treasure one might think. One tobacconist explains it thus: when Castro took over, many of the most skilled Cuban cigar craftsmen went to Nicaragua (and elsewhere), taking a lot of the seed with them. Now, three generations later, perhaps we should be thinking of Nicaragua as the new Cuba. They now have the pride, passion, and skill (not to mention the quality plants and rich soil) once associated with Cuba. Meanwhile, the Cubans are being forced to produce tobacco as fast as possible, under great pressure, resulting in a lot of green cigars that you'd never otherwise smoke.

Are there good Cuban cigars out there? Sure, but you're better off familiarizing yourself with a cigar you can procure regularly and count on to deliver consistently.

CIGARS IN POP CULTURE

I've been a football player and/or coach my entire life, so my cigar-related football memories begin with legendary Steelers owner Art Rooney, who always had a cigar between his teeth, and end with Mike Ditka, who is a cigar enthusiast and who is, well . . . just Ditka. Now that the NFL is sanitized and public-relationed[18] within an inch of its life, these football-related cigar memories are a thing of the past.

Gone are the days of Michael Jordan chomping a stogie[19] in the post-NBA-Finals locker room, moments before being doused with champagne. Gone are the days of Boston Celtics patriarch Red Auerbach and his erstwhile sideline stogie. Because of the late, great Bert Randolph Sugar—he of the suit, fedora, and unlit cigar—boxing and cigars seemed to go hand in hand until Sugar's passing. For Sugar, the cigar was a prop of sorts—a way to underscore a point and a piece of his crafted public persona that added personality to Sugar himself as well as the sport.

The end of the "cigar era" in professional sports, to me, signaled the end of a certain kind of bold, rakish gentleman-athlete who wasn't afraid to occasionally produce a quote or voice an opinion that hadn't previously been vetted by an agent, a lawyer, and twenty-five PR wonks. Sadly, we're living in a post-personality sports society in which it seems athletes are all just saying different versions of the same boring things. As a fan and a writer, this makes me sad. The end, to me, came around 2007 when then-San Francisco 49ers head coach Mike Nolan was told he wasn't allowed to wear a suit on the sidelines (as an homage to his father), because that suit hadn't been produced by then-NFL-uniform-supplier Reebok. *Groan.*

Still, popular culture—specifically films and television—are loaded with cigar references and appearances. The cigar continues to be the choice of fictitious interesting people, if not real interesting people. Here are a few:

Cosmo Kramer, *Seinfeld.* Kramer never worked a real job, was everybody's jocular back-slapping buddy, and smoked cigars all the time. Sounds like a pretty good gig to me. In his tenure as Jerry's neighbor, Kramer produced a coffee-table book about coffee tables, a cologne that smelled like the beach, acted in a Woody Allen movie, and founded Kramerica Industries. And by "produced" and "acted in" and "founded" I of course mean that he didn't actually do any of it. And he pioneered wearing vintage, thrift-store clothing before hipsters started doing it (thereby making it lame). Still, he looked great with a cigar in his hand.

Paulie, from the five *Rocky* movies.
I say five movies because, in my opinion, *Rocky V* never actually existed and was just a bad dream I had once. Paulie used the cigar to affect a weary, downtrodden persona, which seemed to ask the salient question, "What purpose am I serving in life other than to drink beer, be disheveled, and be the guy who lifts the rope up for Rocky when he walks into the ring?" Still, we love Paulie because he's the only guy in those movies who could actually exist in real life.

The Untouchables. One of the great, underrated movies of the 1980s, this Brian DePalma piece starred Sean Connery, Kevin Costner, and Robert DeNiro in a natural turn as Al Capone. I can't begin to catalogue all the reasons why this movie is great, but suffice it to say there are a lot of cigars smoked in it—both by Capone and by the Untouchables as they celebrate their conquests. Just don't make the mistake of looking up the real story of Elliot Ness online because it will depress you. I prefer to remember the unrealistic comic-book version of Ness portrayed in this film.

Tommy Boy. This one is a sleeper cigar hit. You think to yourself, "I'm in the mood for a classic, slapstick '90s comedy the likes of which are no longer seen today—an era in which quote/unquote comedy consists of Zach Galifinakis

(SIC, probably) movies in which buffoonish 30-something bro-guys make moral shipwreck of their lives in a way that's supposed to be quote/unquote "funny." And then you watch *Tommy Boy* and discover a.) The slimy Rob Lowe villain smokes cigars, and even better, b.) Ray Zelinski, the American Auto Parts King (Dan Aykroyd), smokes cigars as well. Zelinski makes auto parts for the working man, because he *is* a working man. He also drops gigantic weights on Rob Lowe's—er—*area*, and then sends him a bottle of bubbly and ice "for his marbles." What a guy.

Mad Men. From the very first line of dialogue, this show is enveloped in a cloud of mid-century smoke. We'll forgive the fact that it's mostly cigar*ette* smoking because these '60s-era Madison Avenue players keep their cigarettes in metal cases and light them with monogrammed lighters. Still, the men of Sterling Cooper & Whoever Else know that, when you need to celebrate landing that big account or winning an advertising award, the only way to go is to light up a fine cigar and pour a glass of—oh, who are we kidding, there was already a glass of something in their hands.

Lord Grantham. You may think it's a bit, er, iffy for two guys of our stature to spend hours discussing the British costume drama *Downton Abbey*. We do this on a regular basis—but we also box in the ring in Ted's basement and Zach carries a handgun . . . Okay, this isn't sounding any better, and you're right in thinking that Freud would have a field day with all of this (including the cigars). Nevertheless, was there ever a show that more effectively glorifies the act and ethos of cigar smoking? The ethos of course being snobby elitism and conspicuous consumption. There's a solemn ritualism in the way the Crawley men retire to the drawing room for cigars and brandy, all of which comes from a large, properly humidified stash of fine smoking and drinking materials, retrieved by a staff of footmen, valets, and servants. I mean really, Lord Grantham should just roll up the British equivalent of a 100 dollar bill and smoke that.

The A-Team. There were probably more cigars smoked, collectively, during the A-Team's seemingly endless run in the 1980s than on any other television program. I'm sure they weren't high-quality cigars given the fact that *The A-Team* routinely tried to convince us that the safe Hannibal just blew up wasn't made out of plywood painted gray (a dead giveaway being the flying pieces of plywood when the "safe" is blown up). The show also tried to convince us that Dirk Benedict was an actor.

Men and Women. There's a definite gender gap in pop culture vis-à-vis cigars and what they convey about a person. When a man is portrayed smoking a cigar, he's either rich (a la Waring Hudsucker), evil (a la alternate-1985 Biff Tannen), or reckless-but-in-a-cool-way (a la Il Duce). But when women light up a stogie, it always conveys one unified message: she's comfortable breaking convention, she's probably cool enough to be "one of the guys" in any given gathering, but she also looks amazing as she smokes, which somehow reinforces her femininity (e.g. Robin Scherbatsky, Salma Hayek, Toni Braxton, Catherine Zeta-Jones, etc.)

This old publicity shot for Gut Check Press betrays a couple of iffy mixed-fill cigars, which have been smoked too hot and tapped to death. Shame on us.

C.S. LEWIS

Lewis is the reason most seminarians go through a "pipe phase." They see how thoughtful the pipe made Lewis look and they're convinced they can pull it off . . . if they can just keep the ضغع thing lit. Lewis did love his pipe, but he was at least as fond of cigarettes (there's no accounting for taste). And, while he may have sort of been a universalist and held to some questionable views on the afterlife, Lewis was undeniably a gifted and challenging Christian thinker worth reading and wrestling with.

"The pipe gives the wise man time to think and the fool something to stick in his mouth."

-C.S. Lewis

 MORE GREAT MOMENTS IN LITERATURE AND FILM IF A MAIN CHARACTER WAS REPLACED BY *CIGAR AFICIONADO'S* JAMES SUCKLING

The Blind Side

Instead of taking underprivileged football prodigy Michael Oher into their spare bedroom, James Suckling and his family decide to just knock out a wall and make the humidor a little bit bigger—resulting in a really great humidor but rendering the story that much less inspirational.

Titanic

In the climactic romantic moment of the film, as Suckling and the Kate Winslet character retreat to the hull of the ship to make out in an abandoned car, Suckling, before making out, exclaims, "I must first smoke a Montecristo Reserva Negra." She rolls her eyes and chews her nails, before saying, "I think we just hit an iceberg and the ship is flooding," to which Suckling replies, "Oh, no big deal, I can just re-light when we get in the lifeboat."

The Hunger Games

Heroine Katniss Everdeen, severely dehydrated and sleep-deprived after 48 hours in the arena, stumbles upon the prone body of her friend Peeta Mellark (Suckling). "What are you doing?" Katniss asks, to which Peeta replies, "I've covered myself in mud and moss in an effort to hide from a rival tribe . . . and I'm also making a list of the best wine and cigar pairings to enjoy in a survival setting. I'm also bleeding to death from this wound in my thigh."

CIGAR SIZES AND SHAPES

So you've got down color and filler, flavor and body. Here's where things seem to get complicated (because of the seemingly unending cigar types out there; see the next page for just a sampling). But really, it's simple. Once you identify the basic convention (length × ring gauge + shape = *Some Awesome Spanishy-Sounding Name*), it's all cream cheese.

Let's start with size. Cigar types are defined first and foremost by ring gauge (the diameter of the stick) and cigar length (in inches, generally, from cap to foot). For example, a Robusto is 5 × 50 (pronounced five by fifty) because it is five inches long with a ring gauge of fifty.

Ring gauge is not counter-intuitive like it is with shotgun gauge; with cigars, the higher the number, the fatter the stogie. The unit here is 1/64 of an inch (i.e., a 64 gauge cigar would be one inch in diameter. It would also be a silly novelty item you bought in the gift shop at Six Flags). If related apart from length, ring gauge is sometimes indicated with a null set symbol (i.e., Ø55).

So that's any cigar's size in just two numbers. Add the shape, wrapper shade, and type of fill, and whether or not you know the specific cigar by name, you can know just about everything you need to in very few words.

Cigar Shapes

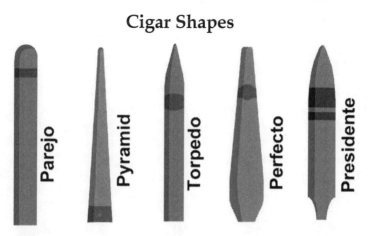

Parejo Pyramid Torpedo Perfecto Presidente

Some Common Cigar Sizes

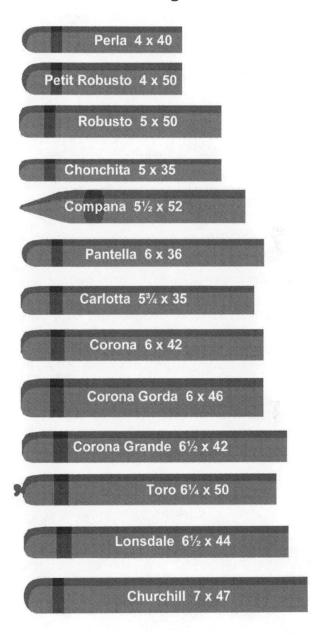

Perla 4 x 40

Petit Robusto 4 x 50

Robusto 5 x 50

Chonchita 5 x 35

Compana 5½ x 52

Pantella 6 x 36

Carlotta 5¾ x 35

Corona 6 x 42

Corona Gorda 6 x 46

Corona Grande 6½ x 42

Toro 6¼ x 50

Lonsdale 6½ x 44

Churchill 7 x 47

Smoking Lounge Etiquette

This book is not interested in the minutiae of protocol in exclusive cigar clubs where an ordinary office drone or suburban dad would feel eternally out of place. If you're part of such a club, you don't need us to help you blend.

No, our kind of smoking lounge lets you be who you are, come as you are (within reason), and relax as you smoke. That said, you don't want to stand out in a bad way or detract from the enjoyment of your fellow patrons.

To that end, here are some habits to avoid in the interest of not becoming "that guy:"

Being a Lounge Lizard.

The lounge lizard spends hours a day in the comfy leather chairs, but does not buy anything. Some days he doesn't smoke at all. Other days, he brings in his own cigars. He might glom on to other people's conversations or he might loudly "close deals" on his cellphone. Does your favorite smoke club have a lounge lizard? If no one comes to mind, take a moment to consider whether it might be you. It's never too late to repent.

Trying to be the snobbiest cigar snob in the room.

Do you talk about smoking "hundred-year-old Cubans?" Do you always have an opinion on everyone else's smoke? Do you absolutely *have to* work Spanish terms and technical language into every cigar conversation? Do you memorize cigar reviews from magazines and try to pass them off as your own? If so, realize that everyone else in the lounge wants you to shut up.

Hiding your ignorance behind lingo and posturing.

Sure, the male ego is notorious for not wanting to ask directions, but if you're new to cigars or don't know that much about them, resist the urge to fake it. As soon as you start asking the shop owner, "Do you have anything with Ecuadorian leaf?" he knows that you're a neophyte. Instead of playing the poseur, make your tobacconist your best friend. Assuming you're in a real cigar shop and not a discount tobacco store (i.e., the smoker's version of Seven-Eleven), your tobacconist is an expert in his field and is there to help guide you into the most enjoyable smoking experience possible. Make the most of that relationship.

Making Chauvinistic Assumptions.

Speaking of male egos, we've heard many a story of men walking right past female tobacconists in order to ask less-knowledgeable males for help choosing a cigar. (This has been known to happen at Timothy's Fine Cigars, where owner Emily McMann and manager Rowan Cooper—both incredibly knowledgeable about all kinds of cigars—are occasionally given the cold shoulder by male patrons in desperate need of their cigar expertise, simply because they are pretty, young, and female.)

We implore you: don't be that guy. Yes, we love that smoking is masculine and old school, but that doesn't mean we want to recreate social dynamics from fifty years ago.

Being an expert on everything.

Whatever is being discussed amidst the smoke today, do you suddenly know everything there is to know on the subject? Whether it's cars, horseback riding, the French Revolution, or nuclear physics? This is a very toxic (yet sadly common) dynamic to introduce to the lounge and is often observed among lounge lizards, as it falls in line with their stated mission of killing all conversation and driving away real customers.

Taking cigars you haven't bought out of the cellophane.

You're not exactly breaking a seal, so it's no big deal, right? Wrong. This is tackier than opening a bag of chips at a convenience store and then deciding you don't want them after all and putting them back on the shelf. Your tobacconist will not be able to sell that cigar. Don't do this. If you want to know what lies beneath that cellophane, just ask.

Smelling the cigars.

This is an instant giveaway that you know nothing about smoking like a gentleman. First off, the smell of a cigar's wrapper tells you very little about how it will smoke. The blend of the filler is what matters most and, as such, the only way to know how it will taste and smell when smoked is to light it up. Sure, we've all seen movies where the fat, rich man decadently sniffs his stogie before igniting it. But here's the thing: that's already *his stogie*. There's nothing ruder in a tobacco shop than the guy who puts his grubby fingers on a fine cigar, runs it under his snotty nose, and then puts it back in the box for someone else to eventually buy and place in his own mouth. Yuck.

PIOUS X

During the early years of the Modernist-Fundamentalist debates within the liberalizing Proestant denominations, there was a pope, Pious X, who was fighting his own battle against modernizing tendencies in the Catholic Church. Pious was conservative, kind, and compassionate, which we dig. And while we are less than thrilled with his devotion to Mary, we love that Pope Pious X (now, St. Pious X in Catholic circles) was a lover of fine cigars. The story is often told (though likely apocryphal) that Pious X once summoned a bishop in order to rebuke him for sinning with women and drink. As a gesture of kindness, he began the meeting by offering the man a fine cigar from the papal humidor (papal humidor!). The bishop, thinking it was a test, declined, saying he had no such vice, to which the pope replied:

If it were a vice, I would not have offered it to you.

SLOWER AND SANER: ON PIPES, ROCK-STARDOM, AND JODY DAVIS

"Don't mind the naked black guy in the hallway," Jody Davis says, as we make our way through a dark passage to the back of the Newsboys' tour bus in Saginaw, Michigan.

"I get that all the time in my line of work," I reply, which is not-untrue of sports writing.

The Newsboys are a CCM pop juggernaut, having launched in Australia, but garnering critical and commercial success stateside in the 1990s. Jody Davis is their lead guitar player. The black guy, in this case, is Michael Tait, formerly of DC Talk and now the lead singer. Outside there are several thousand sweaty evangelicals in lawn chairs waiting to scream for four middle-aged men. The oddness of the scene hasn't escaped Davis. Rather, it is just part of the job.

It's odd, spending time with middle-aged rock stars. The tour bus seems like an appropriate locale for people in their twenties, not so much men with families in their forties. But the thin, dark-bearded Davis turns to pipe-making to help wile away some of the long hours on the road.

"I started playing guitar because I loved music, and with pipes it was the same thing," Davis explains. "In the years before eBay I was big into antiquing on the road. Wherever we had a tour stop I'd find antique stores and estate sales. I started learning about the estate market and antique pipes. I fell in love with the different shapes and wood."

Like most of us, Davis was drawn to the aesthetics, culture, and pace of pipe smoking. "When I first started smoking we had this C.S. Lewis book club in Nashville called 'Inklings,' where we'd smoke pipes and discuss books and theology. Lighting and smoking a pipe helps you to relax and wind down. It helps me to do my reading, and have consistent quiet-times of study. I think it has a tendency to help people who are a little ADD—it's essentially relaxing but it also keeps the mind engaged."

Sometime in the mid-90s Davis bought his first pipe kit and whittled out his first pipe. He then started chasing down higher-quality briar and stem material, and made a pipe that caught the attention of a buyer for a high-end pipe shop in Nashville called "Uptown." "He said, 'Man, this is pretty good'" Davis recalls. "He created a lot of hype for my pipes which I then had to live up to." Davis sought guidance and inspiration from the Danish pipe-masters, who at the time had a corner on the world's high-end pipe market.

Davis explains that the creativity involved in pipe-making is different than the kind that is required for collaborative efforts like songwriting, recording and touring. "I'm basically an introvert," he explains, "which is strange for this line of work [rock-star]. I live for the solitary day in the shop. It's all your own. It's fun to see something through entirely from start to finish."

However, human nature being what it is, there are many of the same dramas and pressures in both industries.

"Everyone's a critic," he says with a smile. "In the pipe community there are lots of chat rooms and lots of dramas." As a result, Davis keeps his online presence to a minimum, as a way of protecting the joy of pipe smoking, but also as a means of managing both worlds—music and pipes. We spend a moment bemoaning the fact that the Internet has changed, well, everything in both of Davis's industries.

"Kids used to buy entire records," he says. "Musicians used to be able to trace their musical influences through bands from the past. Now a kid says, 'I like The Killers, so I'll make a band that sounds like The Killers." Everyone, it seems, is looking for the next 99 cent download hit, rather than the cohesive, coherent album.

All of which only serves to build our appreciation for pipes and cigars—neither of which have changed much. The Internet has primarily become a venue by which we love *ourselves.* Pipe smoking is about loving something else. It's about cuts of tobacco. The size of the bowl. The rate of one's breathing. It's a challenge—more so than cigars—but the best kind of challenge.

"I've always tried to keep the two worlds fairly separate," he says of music and pipes. "But I've got lots of pastors, monks, and fans of the band who are also pipe customers."

Davis's level of production varies each year, based partly on customer demand, partly on family, and partly on Newsboys recording and touring demands. Davis took a five-year hiatus from the band a while back, in order to stay home to care for a daughter with severe disabilities. It was during those years at home that his pipe-making prowess grew, along with his productivity.

"I was reminded that guitar-playing, pipe-making and the Newsboys is *not* my identity," he says. "My identity is as a child of God. Stepping away from music was difficult because of the fear of the unknown. It was risky. It took a year and a half to really build my pipe business. The Danes had developed high-end pipes . . . but I wanted to take American pipe-making to the next level.

"It was a real God-send," Davis says of the pipe-making, which allowed an outlet for his creativity apart from music. "He brought that into my life and allowed me to be home for five years, which was where I needed to be."

There is something of the ancient in pipe-making and pipe smoking. It's an excuse to appreciate and delve deeply into history. "I love the history," Davis says. "I collect old pipe advertisements out of different ads. I've got Dunhill pipes from the 1920s. It's the kind of thing that you take good care of and pass on."

It's so completely rare for any man to be "world-class" at anything, much less two things. I reflect on this as Davis and I wrap our interview, and as I step out of the climate-controlled enclave of the tour bus. In a few hours, Davis will meet an audience that knows him only as a guitar player. I feel fortunate to have connected with him as a pipe smoker and artisan

"It was months and months of smoking a pipe before I had 'that' moment," he says. "The moment with the right tobacco, the right rhythm. I just said 'Oh man, this is awesome.' Pipe smoking is for people who want to reach back for something slower, and saner."

For more information on Jody Davis, or to purchase a pipe, visit www.jodydavispipes.com

49

CIGARS, TYPEWRITERS, SUITS, VINYL: IN PRAISE OF THINGS THAT ARE OLD

It's no secret that we live in a culture that is obsessed with new. A few years ago, it seemed to be a priority to get a cell phone that was as tiny as possible. Now, the priority is to have a "phone," which is really a slightly scaled-down tablet computer from which you can run your entire life, and by your "entire life" I mean your Facebook™, Twitter™, LinkedIn™, Pinterest™, and Instagram™ accounts. The fact that this trend has not only *not missed* ministry, but seems to be central to it (they'll know us by our angry blogs), is also no secret to anyone.

We are, of course, smug and disdainful when it comes to such things and, in this, we are old men who are both turning into our fathers. That said, cigars fit well with our "appreciation of old" ethos.

Things we love:

1. **Suits** - Every man should own a few high-quality, well-fitting suits. Sadly, we live in a society where people don't dress up to go out to nice restaurants. Not so for Gut Check. We suit up regularly, and you should too. If you're the kind of guy who wears sweat pants to restaurants stop reading this immediately and go buy a suit. Do it.

   Suits hearken back to a day when men were men, and when working was infinitely respectable. Back when Dad put on his fedora on the way out the door, and back when people wore jackets and ties to sporting events rather than in present-day stadiums, where grown men wear jerseys and paint their faces. And sometimes their huge stomachs. Now I'm ranting.

2. **Hats** - Speaking of which, there's really no good reason not to wear a classy, timeless hat when you're dressing up a bit. Do you know why everybody gets all wistful and yearning and almost-jealous about things like the early seasons of *Mad Men*, those hundred-year-old mug shots on the wall in that prohibition-themed restaurant, and every period movie set between 1890 and 1960 (especially those starring Johnny Depp)? It really just boils down to one thing: the fact that every male is always wearing a slick-looking hat (usually cocked slightly) or holding said hat (along with a hand-carved tippling cane) or hanging it, smoothly, on a hat rack. (How men wore hats all the time in an era when they also applied what was essentially petroleum jelly to every strand of hair is beyond me.) The point is, we get all bummed out that we no longer wear hats when nothing at all is keeping us from wearing hats.

   If you'd like to become a hat-wearer, you've got two options the way we see it: 1.) You can jump in all at once like Neil Caffrey or Bert Sugar; put on a fedora, stick a Montecristo between your teeth, and never remove either until you take the big dirt nap, or 2.) You can take it slow. If you go for the second option, a good first step is to stop wearing backwards baseball caps, and then stop wearing baseball caps at all. (You're not ten years old, after all.) Wait for cold weather and gradually introduce a fedora (or maybe a bowler if that's more your speed). Before long, you'll be at home under your new hat, and probably turning phrase and oozing style like a character in a Humphrey Bogart movie.

3. **Typewriters** - Nearly every great work of literature was written on a typewriter. The gentle clack of keys. The neat pile of paper stacked next to the typewriter in a box. A little ink on your fingers after changing the ribbon. The fact that JD Salinger used a typewriter.

Other great things about typewriters: The lack of Facebook, Twitter, Pinterest, blogs, and Internet porn. Save your Covenant Eyes subscription and just get a typewriter.

4. **Vinyl Records** - I know I'm veering into "obnoxious hipster" territory here, but I love vinyl records. I love the gentle crackle the needle makes when first grooved into a new (old) record. I love that every crummy antique store (see: antiquing, and how it's awesome) has a box of vinyl in the corner someplace with a trove of cheap treasures. Vinyl hearkens back to a day when people didn't start diddling their iPhones to find their "music collection." I want my music collection to be in a pile on my office floor, next to my stereo. I want big cover art and liner notes. I want vinyl.

5. **Ashtrays** - One of the hidden advantages to being a cigar smoker is all the little accessories that go with the hobby, not the least of which is the great ashtray potential. There are elaborate '50s-era floor-models, where at the push of a button the ashes are magically whisked away to the . . . uh . . . bottom of the ashtray. There are glass models that remind us of old hotels and old restaurants. There are even the cheap, plastic, diner-style ashtrays that look awesome and retro now that it's illegal to smoke everywhere.

6. **Matchbook Collecting** - Remember when restaurants and hotels used to give out matchbooks? You could have a bowl or ashtray in your house overflowing with multi-colored, multi-logoed matchbooks showing the design aesthetics of their various entities and providing an archive of all the interesting places you've been.

Now . . . I guess there's Facebook for that? Meh.

7. **Shaving Implements** - Is there any more embarrassing yardstick for the decline of manliness in America than TV commercials for space-aged disposable razors that feature seven blades, something called a "sensitivity strip," and a network of little plastic springs and bands, which work in tandem with some greenish-blue gel to make sure your face looks downright preadolescent?

The very fact that you picked up this book tells us you're better than that—meaning you recognize that shaving is an essential part of being a man. It's this understanding that leads many men to spring for a hot lather dispenser to try and replicate the hot shave of an old fashioned barber shop. The really serious shaver may even invest in a straight razor and strap. The most important shaving apparatus a man can own, though, is the brush and bowl (especially an antique one). When you start the day by whipping soap into a lather with a shaving brush, knowing that the competition is smearing some greenish ectoplasm-in-a-can all over his cheeks, you may as well just skip right to the victory cigar.

8. **Old Books** - Caveat: We both have Kindles and most Gut Check products are packaged for electronic delivery. But that said, old books are *way* better. For me, there are few things more enjoyable than hitting my favorite used bookstore (Curious Book Shop, East Lansing) and browsing the old novels and magazines there. When you buy a book they ring it up on an old-school cash register and put it in an old-school paper bag. Books are ownable and archiveable. They invite discussion and opinions around the house. A great cover design is pure art. These are all things we miss with electronic delivery. When I pass down my book collection to my kids I want to do more than hand them a microchip.

9. **Retro Phones** - Remember when people couldn't get a hold of you all the time? I do. It was great (see: introvert). I remember when evenings and weekends weren't ruined by the ability to check email on the phone to get the inevitable piece of publishing industry bad news that inevitably comes at 4:59 PM on Friday. I remember when texts weren't misinterpreted because there weren't any texts. I remember when I was actually present in the moment I was in, because there weren't texts and emails and eBay to check on my mobile device.

Great Retro Phones: Black desk phones, wall-mounted kitchen phones, rotary-dial phones, crappy '80s cordless phones (the white ones with the telescoping antennae), the helmet phones they used to use at the NFL draft (I coveted, and still covet, one of these), the crappy football phone that came with my Sports Illustrated subscription as a kid.

That sound you hear is me backing over my iPhone with my Cadillac.

10. **Cadillacs**

J.R.R. TOLKIEN

Along with C.S. Lewis, Tolkien was a member of the Inklings, a literary group who met, among other places, in pubs and classrooms to discuss what they were writing, as well as enjoying a drink and smoke together.

"After some time he felt for his pipe. It was not broken, and that was something. Then he felt for his pouch, and there was some tobacco in it, and that was something more. Then he felt for matches and he could not find any at all, and that shattered his hopes completely."

— *The Hobbit* [20]

CUTTERS, ETC.

Part of the draw (see what I did there?) of cigar smoking for men is the plethora of accessories. It's like stereo equipment, gun-cleaning kits, and football gear—it gives us an excuse to buy a toy box and fill it up. One of the most essential cigar accessories is, of course, the cutter.

We're gonna go ahead and say this right off the bat, even though we wish it went without saying: anything that doesn't need to be cut (i.e. anything with a wood or plastic tip or machine-made with a hole in the cap) *should never be smoked*. That said, with the huge variety of cutting and poking implements out there, which way should you go?

Well, you can get a crappy plastic guillotine cutter for a buck at your local cigar store. But don't do that. Seriously, don't. You're going to chew up the ends of your cigars before you even stick them in your mouth and have all sorts of blockages and funky draws thereafter.

The ultimate cutter, in our book, is the multi-cut cigar store apparatus (actually called by a variety of names, including "Quad Tabletop Cutter"). You've seen these: they have four different holes, each representing a different cut, and a large lever, which draws a blade across all four major cut-types, cutting your cigar (or cigars, as I suppose you could do more than one at a time with such a device—but why would you want to?). You can buy these new for about forty bucks on several cigar-themed websites, but they're almost all chromish, space-age-looking things. We'd much rather own an antique tabletop cutter that was once mounted in a cigar shop or old-timey drug store. Speaking of which, the big, table-mounted cigar lighters ("I wish I had a million dollars. *Hot dog!*") are also an ever-elusive, but hotly sought-after commodity for the cigar-smoking gentleman. Sadly, neither of us has yet to find an affordable and not-busted one of either of these for sale.[21]

If you can't find one either (or even if you can, since you'll need something portable at some point), a good place to start would be a nice surgical steel, self-sharpening double-blade guillotine cutter. Or a high-quality example of one of the following:

V-Cut: The best way to go with parejos, this cutter slices out a slit in the cap of the cigar. To increase airflow, cut once, turn ninety degrees, and cut again, making a cross. Now smoke your cigar to the glory of God.

Guillotine: These operate just like the name implies and come in either single- or double-bladed versions. Guillotines create a straight-cut and are good for anything with a tapered end (like a torpedo or perfecto). The sad thing about this is that you lose the cap and any filler contained therein right off the bat, which becomes cigar that you paid for, but won't be smoking.

Scissor Cutters: The downside here is that these equally resemble a.) some 19th century torture device developed for use in "Lunatic Asylums" and b.) something a cop would find while tossing the backpack of a "reefer" enthusiast. All the same, they're great for saving a cigar you want to finish later, as you won't need to try and fit a burning cigar through the hole of a guillotine cutter without burning yourself or damaging the wrapper. One word of caution, though: if they are even beginning to dull, scissor cutters will rip your cigar *apart*.

Punch: This clever little device punctures the wrapper, binder, and filler, removing a small "bullet" of tobacco." (As you would imagine, you cannot use this on any sort of tapered-cap cigar). The upside is that it creates good draw and can be very convenient (it will fit on your key chain without raising eyebrows). The downside is that it's very easy to burst the end and ruin the cigar. Punches must be incredibly sharp (which cheap ones never are) to avoid popping the side of the cigar's cap.

Whatever you use, be careful; you may be tempted to cut the shoulder (where the cap meets the body). Bad move! If you remove the whole cap (which has been glued on with vegetable-based adhesive) your cigar will begin uncurling and exploring the space of your hand in a very undesirable way. Remember, you can always cut more, but you can never un-cut.

What About Awls?

We've talked about implements for the initial cutting, but what about those long, pointy tools designed to increase the draw of the cigar by hollowing out a spot down the middle?

Actually, "designed" is probably too strong a word—more like "decaled." I once purchased one of these "cigar awls" from a smoke shop, only to have a friend point out that it was a regular $1 bargain bin awl with a sticker stuck on it. (The sticker said "Maverick" and was apparently worth $10.) My friend mocks me to this day for having purchased such a device, which has more potential to pop the side of your cigar wrapper than anything else. I still have the "mini-awl" that came with it, and very occasionally pull it out to remove a blockage in a cigar. But ultimately, an experienced smoker observes this rule of thumb:

If you have to poke it, don't smoke it.

THE HOLY SPIRIT AND THE AMERICAN SPIRIT: A PROFILE OF TIMOTHY SOCIER, CIGAR SHOP OWNER

Timothy Socier, proprietor of Timothy's Fine Cigars in Bay City, MI was once a plastics engineer. In that role, he was responsible for the creation of the little valve thing at the end of a Gatorade bottle that allows an athlete to lay the bottle on its side without all the Gatorade spilling out. He's the reason why these bottles are routinely tossed around sidelines. He also designed the valve on Heinz Ketchup squeeze bottles and several other things in your house right now.

More importantly, he was instrumental in the creation of a similar but more complicated valve on the inside of NASA space helmets which allows astronauts to drink water from their suits without the risk of drowning in that water in the event of the water spilling inside their helmet. In layman's terms, the Socier Closer makes it so the water doesn't ever spill inside the helmet.

"Did you get rich making those things?" I asked him one day, over cigars.

"No but I got a nice plaque," he replied. Imagine an arrangement of deep burgundy leather chairs set in an elliptical pattern. Imagine Zach and I on one side, with Tim and a few other people on the other side. I asked how a successful plastics engineer ended up a tobacconist (we'll get to the importance of that particular term later).

He replied that he had been flying to Wisconsin on Monday of each week and working through Friday for a client, away from his family. One night, his supervisor took him to an upscale cigar bar in Milwaukee called The Havana Lounge, where he enjoyed his first premium cigar. "It was a spiritual experience," he said without a trace of irony. "I fell in love with it."

His love was, however, momentarily tempered by a moment of reality at another smoke shop in Bay City. "I came back from the Milwaukee trip and wanted to try another premium cigar," he remembered. "I walked into this place and there was an old, wrinkly lady sitting at the counter smoking a cigarette (ed. Note: this isn't done in true cigar lounges) that had this long ash hanging off of it. I asked her to help me pick out a cigar to smoke and she walked into the humidor and literally threw a cigar at me. I said to myself, 'I can do better than this.'"

Socier then embarked on a years-long cigar journey that included OCD-ishly studying tobacco, cigar-making, and cigar-licensure before opening a premium cigar shop that initially operated out of his family's living room.

"It was definitely strange to be watching television in our bathrobes in the evening, only to have somebody ring the doorbell and want to buy a cigar," he recalled. One of the other smokers in the club asked Socier's wife what she thought of the transition from weekly paycheck to freelance tobacconist. She tucked her bare feet into the burgundy leather, thought for a minute, and said, "I told him to go for it."

Socier's transition from the futuristic (plastics) to the semi-ancient (cigars and tobacco) is an interesting one. "Cigars are still made by hand, just like they were centuries ago," he explained. "A father teaches his son, who in turn teaches *his* son. Three hundred pairs of hands go into making this work of art [the cigar]. It's a plastic, disposable world we live in. The cigar shop experience should be different."

With that ethos at heart, Socier created the atmosphere we enjoy today. It's an environment that has at times been a spiritual haven for customers, and for the owner himself.

"My wife and I had been burned by a church," Socier said, "and we had tried attending a handful of others, but couldn't find anything with substance. We were kind of done with the whole thing. Then we suddenly found ourselves in the middle of a crisis, facing the possibility of losing the shop, our home, everything."

"I was about ready to end my life," recalled Socier, emotional. "I remember, a former pastor of mine came by the shop to drop something off and I invited him to come in and sit down with me."

Despite Tim's state of mind and need for a listening ear and biblical counsel, his one-time pastor declined the invitation—not wanting, he explained, to be seen darkening the door of such an establishment. This seemed to confirm some of Tim's doubts about the Church and even his faith.

Enter Pastor Todd Gould, an ordained minister in the Evangelical Free Church and regular patron at Timothy's Fine Cigars, who offered Tim his ear, his counsel, and his prayers. Over the course of weeks and months, Pastor Todd sat, smoked, and talked with his friend and tobacconist regularly, leading him back again and again to the Loving God who had, in Christ, paid the price for Timothy's sins and brought him from death to life.

"I rediscovered my faith over cigars and scotch," he proclaimed, smiling wryly. And Tim's not the only one who has. "We host a Tuesday night Bible study for people, largely, who would never darken the door of a church. This is a non-traditional venue. Very relaxed. Non-judgmental."

He led us down a back set of stairs and into a basement, where folding tables adorned with copies of the *Apologetics Study Bible* and an "Ask the Pastor" jar sat in the middle of the room. It's this space that has, Socier said, "Saved lives."

I ask Socier if this—the lounge—is how he envisioned it, and if he still loves the cigar business.

"It is indeed a business," he says. "We're not all family. Some in the cigar world only care about making money. And in the community, we're shunned by a certain set. Sometimes people walk by here, see the smoke *inside,* and start coughing just to make a point. And, of course, ObamaCare is gonna punish us."

"But we offer a unique product and a unique atmosphere," he continued. "We bring something really great to our community, and have brought together people I would never have otherwise met, from all walks of life.

"I still love it. I love talking to people. I love coming to work each day. Smoking a cigar, to me, is still about celebrating life. It's an hour of stepping off the world, to celebrate the good things in life."

Dealing with the Nanny State

Tim is frank about his struggles with the nanny state and its inexplicable campaign against above-board, state-revenue-generating cigar shops. Michigan is one of the worst offenders in this regard, but several other states are giving her a run for her money. North Dakota recently made it illegal to smoke in any public building, Tim tells us, even in a cigar shop. A friend of Tim's and fellow cigar shop owner in the Peace Garden State now leases the building next door to his customers so they can have a place to enjoy a smoke and a beverage (as it is a privately owned building). In California, one can no longer smoke on public sidewalks. And Alaska is shooting for some sort of *theater of the absurd* distinction with its ever-rising, ceilingless tobacco tax.

For his part, Tim has felt the noose slowly tighten over the years. He was recently told he can't have a coffee maker for the patrons to use, because he is not licensed to serve food.

In theory, this should apply across the board to funeral homes, banks, and hair salons, but only seems to be an issue in tobacco shops.

In addition, the rules have changed for how he may present and sell his products. Mixing two blends of pipe tobacco (i.e. a little cherry and a little vanilla in a third "cherry vanilla" canister) is now considered "manufacturing" and can land the proprietor in a whole heap of trouble. The store's former practice of having a local printer produce bands for their house brand cigars (which were then affixed by hand in-house) is also now forbidden, as it too somehow allegedly constitutes "manufacturing."

These absurd regulations drive many otherwise laid-back businessmen to drink—er—smoke. Says Tim, "This country was founded by men willing to accept the consequences of their choices. The Nanny State turns that on its head and says, *You need me to think for you.*"

So how does a cigar store deal with it? Well, some throw caution to the wind and just ignore the problem. We've been in some shops where they try and skirt the law and straddle the line, all the while risking their shop's license. And Tim? While he doesn't like it, he complies nonetheless. At the same time, the Michigan Cigar Association (of which he is a member) is pushing for laws that will differentiate between cigar shops and the kind of discount tobacco-slash-bong dispensaries that specialize in papers and rolling machines as a way to avoid paying tobacco tax on cigarettes.

And what can the average smoker do when it comes to the nanny state? Not much. Tim's advice: make sure to take long breaks from the news. "The government wants to think for us," he says. "They want to stress us out until we say, 'Forget it; it's not worth it.' I've been on a news fast for months now, and I've never felt better."

KARL BARTH

Dr. Karl Barth is either loved or hated (or kind of hate-loved) by most theologians. He certainly had some issues, both theologically and personally (*ahem-Charlotte- ahem!*), but his drive to go up against the likes of Bultmann and Brunner has endeared him to many conservative Christians, even those who reject neo-orthodoxy in general. His multi-volume *Church Dogmatics* is well-known for sitting, unread, on pastors' shelves, looking cool.

Barth enjoyed smoking both cigars and pipe. And he was one who sent a cigar to Bonhoeffer in prison.

Which is awesome.

THE DAILY TELEGRAPH SCANDAL

Our recurring anthem of "smoking to the glory of God" finds its origins in a public controversy that played out in 1874.[22] It involved Spurgeon and a godly American Baptist pastor and evangelist named George Pentecost (a frequent collaborator with D.L. Moody). Spurgeon had invited Rev. Pentecost, who was visiting England, to share the pulpit at Spurgeon's church, the Metropolitan Tabernacle. Their plan was that Spurgeon would establish a thesis (in this case, the danger of "little sins") and Brother Pentecost would illustrate and apply it, which he did by referring to his own struggle with smoking, an addiction which God had allowed him to conquer. He went beyond that, though, and railed against the evils of tobacco generally—and cigars in particular— whether smoked in moderation or excess.[23]

At the close of the sermon, Rev. Spurgeon took to the pulpit and respectfully added that, while he agreed in principle with the point Pentecost had made, he did not believe cigar smoking to be a sin in itself and, in fact, by the grace of God, he hoped to enjoy a good cigar before going to bed that night.[24] His attitude and intent in making these closing comments was immediately analyzed from all angles and hotly debated. *Christian World* magazine described Spurgeon as rising to speak "with a somewhat playful smile"[25] and *The Daily Telegraph* had him speaking "with a twinkling eye," a claim which Spurgeon himself vehemently denied in a letter to the newspaper in question, taking offense at the implication that he would ever speak flippantly from the pulpit. "Indeed, I did nothing of the kind," he insisted, adding, "I was rather too much in earnest than too little."[26]

The *Christian World's* account of Spurgeon's remarks was a bit fuller than the *Telegraph's* and makes it clear that Spurgeon was defending something much larger than his own pet habit:

"If anybody can show me in the Bible the command, 'Thou shalt not smoke,' I am ready to keep it; but I haven't found it yet. I find ten commandments, and it's as much as I can do to keep them; and I've no desire to make them into eleven or twelve.

"The fact is, I have been speaking to you about real sins, not about listening to mere quibbles and scruples. At the same time, I know that what a man believes to be sin becomes a sin to him, and he must give it up . . . Why, a man may think it a sin to have his boots blacked. Well, then, let him give it up, and have them whitewashed. I wish to say that I'm not ashamed of anything whatever that I do, and I don't feel that smoking makes me ashamed, and therefore I mean to smoke to the glory of God."[27]

In his initial letter to the *Daily Telegraph,* Spurgeon was both disappointed that such a controversy had erupted over nothing and unwilling to be guilted into giving up his cigars by prominent Christians who certainly did not fit the bill of "the weaker brother."

The controversy raged on for weeks in the pages of the *Christian World* and *Daily Telegraph* as well as in parlors and narthexes on both sides of the Atlantic, drawing in many church leaders.

One Londoner, a W.M. Hutchings, even went so far as to write and distribute a tract against Spurgeon, painting himself and his fellow anti-tobacco and tee-totaling crusaders as victims of slander and lamenting Spurgeon's use of his influence to "confirm . . .self-indulgence" in the young men of his congregation—the kind of self-indulgence which was "disgustingly offensive to hundreds of their fellow worshipers"—and assuming that Spurgeon's example would cause poor men to buy tobacco with money that should have gone toward food, clothing, and education for their children (thus leaving said children naked, hungry, and stupid.)[28]

The name of the tract? *Smoking to the Glory of God.*

MUSINGS ON CIGARS BY A NON-SMOKER

by Frank Turk

If you're a member of the Gut Check Army, you know that no Gut Check book would be complete without world-famous blogger (and menace that must be stopped) Frank Turk weighing in on the topic at hand. True, Turk has never taken Ted and Zach up on their offer of after-dinner cigars, but that would never stop him from waxing eloquent, would it?

My first exposure to someone smoking a stogie was seeing Ben Grimm and/or Nick Fury chewing on a black smear of smoldering tobacco on the pages of Marvel comics. Well, that's actually a lie, but it sounds like something I would say, doesn't it? My actual first-person first experience with cigars was, as a kid, the utterly-stank miasma of the 50-cent cigars my mother's Uncle Bubby (honest to God) used to smoke when he came to visit us each summer.

Bubby was a Navy vet, and he picked up the habit of chewing a half-lit cigar when he was a sailor. By the smell of it, it didn't seem to matter to him if that thing in his mouth was a burning tamale or a piece of sweaty rope or a piece of retread tire he picked up on the way into town—what mattered, it seemed, was that it was stuck in the left-hand side of his mouth in order to cause him to always speak through a half-wry grimace. Maybe he was practicing for his big break into ventriloquism and he had yet to find his one great wooden-headed companion, but let's be honest: usually he just sounded like he was too bored to open his mouth, so he spoke through his teeth.

My other exposure to smoking was Clint Eastwood in the great '60s and '70s Westerns—although I'm sure the purists will object to calling what he smoked in those movies "cigars." They were more like puggish joints of justice, and in my imagination as I watched *High Plains Drifter* or *Hang 'Em High* with my dad on the black and white TV in the basement, I was certain that whatever Clint was smoking in those movies did not smell like Bubby's burning garbage: I'm sure it smelled like the smoldering pile left after God strikes something with a lightning bolt, plus gunpowder and blood. I'm sure it wasn't a sweet smell, but in some sense it was mouth-watering, like the smell of a burnt offering in the Old Testament.

So I was conflicted by the idea of smoking cigars all the way through college—and in college, we all knew smoking (tobacco) was a medical sin, so only the pre-hipster theater wags would smoke anything, and most of them were smoking clove cigarettes. Because even then I knew the difference between actually doing crazy and stupid things and pretending to do crazy and stupid things, I didn't smoke at all. I was a cigar agnostic for years.

To this day, and I think to my credit, I have still never smoked a cigar in my life—in spite of the endorsement such a thing has from the likes of P.J. O'Rourke, Robert De Niro, Ernest Hemingway, Winston Churchill, Bill Cosby, Rush Limbaugh, Mark Twain, and most importantly: Zach and Ted.

I get it—really. It is a manly thing to do. It looks decadent the way a Harley looks decadent, but somehow the Harley (which costs 1,000 times more than a decent cigar) reflects the poor man's depravity, and the cigar is the rich man's vice. It apparently needs a decent whiskey to go with it to be fully appreciated, and a closed room into which no women can enter. It comes bundled with the kind of laughter which is both knowing and aloof, both well-connected and un-impeachably independent. It speaks to a gentleman's code of ethics in which burning plants and barely-heating a steak are necessary virtues. You can actually tell by the smell of a fellow's library whether or not there's anything worth reading in there.

I get it. There's a reason a cheap cigar is such a callow thing—it's supposed to be the way one shows one's lack of concern for actually burning up a $20 bill, like the way one shows one can walk through a sulfur mine without an air mask. It shouldn't smell like a pipe, a smell which does not offend the wife; it should smell like something musky and muscular and perilous—something you probably can't take into the house. It should have the same effect on women that a loaded gun does: that somehow they would never touch it, but they admire and trust the man who does.

There's something inherently sexist about cigars—and nobody cares. Nobody cares because it's a non-issue, like saying that the human race in not just made up of ambiguous people—it's made up of boys and girls, men and women. And cigars are for men.

And this book about cigars is written by men. I'm not going to talk about whether or not they are having a bromance because (A) that's tawdry and (B) they're smoking cigars, so obviously. Or maybe obviously not—I can't decide. But these fellows box, and build cars from scratch (or nearly), and cannot be cowed by the idea that something may not be daintily polite. There's something oddly steampunk about Ted and Zach which is exactly spot-on for loving cigars. Since they obviously know something about it, I'm going to leave the rest to them.

Frank Turk blogs regularly at http://teampyro.blogspot.com.

CIGAR BRANDS AND WHAT THEY SAY ABOUT YOU

Like most if not all consumer purchases, your cigar brand choices will, ultimately, say something about you. Below we've listed a few cigar brands and what they communicate about the smoker. Buy accordingly!

Cohiba

If you're a high-powered executive in 1997, you probably smoke Cohibas while closing deals, wearing your saddle oxfords, and talking on your gray Motorola flip phone. Cohiba was the overpriced elite cigar of the late-'90s cigar boom and for all my stereotyping above, it's a great smoke! Cohibas go through three fermentation stages (rather than the usual two) and were originally made exclusively for Fidel Castro. I have no doubt that Bernie Madoff probably smoked Cohibas, as did the guys who ruined Enron, as did every greasy bad-guy executive in every late-'90s movie about business. As did Michael Jordan.

You'll be tempted to sort of clutch your Cohiba between your lips as you tee off on the golf course, just like Jordan did. But when you do it you won't be able to keep it lit and it will sort of awkwardly fall out of your mouth at the top of your backswing, causing the rest of your foursome to sort of chuckle at you in embarrassment, which will jeopardize the Business Deal you're trying to close on the golf course thereby eroding the entire Persona you're trying to create vis-à-vis the cigar, the golfing, the saddle oxfords, the BMW you can't afford, etc., which causes everybody in your foursome to realize what you should have realized before you bought the Cohiba and thought about taking it to the golf course and what your wife has always known: You're not Michael Jordan. You'll never make it above middle management. You'll never make partner. Your dad is going to be so disappointed.

Acid

Please take a moment to complete the following quiz.

Do you . . .
- a.) Own a pair of leather pants, unironically?
- b.) Own a purple shirt that is also shiny?
- c.) Zoom down the highway on what is known in the motorcycle community as a "crotch-rocket?"

If you answered "yes" to any of the above, you probably smoke Acid cigars. Acid is the brand that Bobby Brown and Keith Sweat would have smoked in 1988, were they (the cigars) around in 1988.

Esteban Carerras 187

Ever wondered how to capitalize, in a marketing sense, on the police code for murder (187)? That's what this cigar brand boldly (boldly?) did a few years ago. If you own Affliction t-shirts and regularly attend regional-level MMA (aka Mixed Martial Arts, aka Cage Fighting, aka That Thing You Probably Did Once) shows, you probably smoke 187s. You probably also drink Kid Rock's "Badass" American Lager. You probably also enjoyed the movie *Four Brothers*, starring Mark Wahlberg and three other people, a movie whose alternate title was *Pretty Much the Only Bad Movie Mark Wahlberg Has Done in the Last Decade.*[29]

Swisher Sweets

You're 12 and just stole some money from your mom's purse, rode your bike to the gas station, and bought these from the clerk, who sold them to you because you're the most "mature looking" kid in your friend group on account of your scummy semi-moustache. Return the cigars because they suck, shave your moustache, and tell your mom about the money. Seriously. Do it.

Davidoff

If you're a high-powered executive today, you should take care, because the current Presidential administration would like to completely do away with high-powered executives, being that successful businesses are obviously evil, bad for the economy, and can't be trusted. That said, if you buy and sell people for a living, you probably smoke *Davidoffs.* You probably also own a Rolls Royce, several Rolexes, a hot tub, and have two or three secret wives stashed somewhere in the Dakotas. If heaven has a "house" cigar brand, it will be this smooth, creamy, admittedly-overpriced-but-still-wonderful cigar.

Your Local Tobacconist's "House Brand."

If you live in a city with a population of 10,000 or more, odds are good you've got a local tobacconist who not only runs a cigar shop stocked with a variety of brands, but also sells his own cigars. He probably has a guy who rolls them. The guy's name is probably Manny and he is probably (allegedly) from Central America. You've never met the guy and are not sure he exists.

All the same, a bundle of your local smoke shop's house brand will almost always cost you less than the same bundle of your go-to brand. But even if you can find a good long-fill or mixed-fill house brand cigar, it's a lot harder to find one that will be *consistently* good. The other problem with house brand cigars (at least in smaller operations) is that the bands were often printed on an inkjet printer, snipped with scissors, and applied with a glue stick by the store's "intern" (read: the proprietor's girlfriend's nephew). This all gives what should be a refined and sophisticated experience (enjoying a relaxing smoke) a decidedly bush league feel. Remove the band in the privacy of your home before lighting up and you may just be the most economically savvy smoker out there. And don't forget to pick up that three-gallon tub of store-brand mayo at Quantity Plus tonight.

Garcia y Vega

You don't know anything about cigars, but you wish you did. You've heard that fine cigars come from places where Spanish is spoken and so Spanish-sounding names seem like a safe bet. Also the fact that each cigar comes in its own little tube seems *fancy*. And how convenient that you don't need a cigar cutter, as these cigars have been pre-poked at the factory! All this for only *two bucks* a piece?! Wow-ee! Garcia y Vega is counting on people like you to keep them in business. They're counting on the use of *y* instead of *&* to confuse you, which it has. *Are these the cigars they gave out at your cousin's wedding? Because those were pretty good.* (Hint: those were Romeo y Julietas.) *Didn't the clerk at the cigar store recommend these to you as an inexpensive-but-good smoke when you were on vacation?* (Nope, those were Arturo Fuentes). *Why are they* green*?* (See "The Components of a Cigar," page 17.)

You poor thing; you mean well; you just need someone to set you straight. Good thing you picked up this book.

Outlaws (those gnarled cheroot things)

This is the cigar that Clint Eastwood smoked in *The Good, The Bad, and The Ugly*. You buy them in bags, which should tell you everything you need to know. This is the cigar you smoke if you actually are a cigarette smoker. These are a special smoke to enjoy while sitting in your garage next to your requisite red Craftsman tool cabinet and Dallas Cowboys Cheerleader calendar (circa 1989).

A Caution about Buying Online

There are many tobacco vendors and wholesalers who offer boxes, bundles, and assortments of cigars via Internet sales. Some are shady; others can claim with integrity to have been selling cigars by mail for a hundred years. Online purchases can be a great way to stock up your humidor, but be aware: If you are buying tobacco products online in order to save the extra taxes you'd pay at your local shop, what you're doing is probably illegal (unless you claim and pay the sales tax *and* pay the tobacco tax after the fact by going to a state-run website and voluntarily ponying up the cash—which no one has ever actually done). Our state's government has (with cigarettes) subpoenaed sales records and gone after people for exactly that. And, while we cannot speak for every state, odds are good yours has similar rules in place.

Even apart from legal and ethical considerations, a good tobacconist can probably match your online prices anyway. Mr. Dale Foote, my father in law, recently made the switch from Internet to all-local and found that, even with the proper taxes paid on site, his local tobacconist could beat the online prices. He also found a new (and cheaper) go-to smoke in one of his tobacconist's house brands. And his money goes just across the river, rather than across the country.

SPURGEON ON EARLY-MORNING SMOKE

In recording his personal memories of Charles Spurgeon, William Williams relates the following story:

> While Mr. Spurgeon was living at Nightingale Lane, Clapham, an excursion was one day organised by one of the young men's classes at the Tabernacle. The brake with the excursionists was to call for the President on their way to mid-Surrey.
>
> It was a beautiful early morning, and the men arrived in high spirits, pipes and cigars alight, and looking forward to a day of unrestrained enjoyment. Mr. Spurgeon was ready waiting at the gate. He jumped up to the box-seat reserved for him, and looking round with an expression of astonishment, exclaimed: "What, gentlemen! Are you not ashamed to be smoking so early?"
>
> Here was a damper! Dismay was on every face. Pipes and cigars one by one failed and dropped out of sight.
>
> When all had disappeared, out came the President's cigar-case. He lit up and smoked away serenely.
>
> The men looked at him astonished. "I thought you said you objected to smoking, Mr. Spurgeon?" one ventured.
>
> "Oh no, I did not say I objected. I asked if they were not ashamed, and it appears they were, for they have all put their pipes away."
>
> Amid laughter the pipes reappeared, and with puffs of smoke the party went on merrily.[30]

J. GRESHAM MACHEN

Machen has become one of the most celebrated figures in all of wider Reformedom for his stand against Modernism at Princeton, his founding of Westminster Theological Seminary, and his seminal work, *Christianity and Liberalism*. Looking back through history, A.A. Hodge and B.B. Warfield were just sort of warm-up acts for Machen, who was the real deal. And, while Machen was no cigar or pipe smoker, he actually *wished* he had been. While a student at Princeton, he wrote this in a letter to his mother:

"When I think what a wonderful aid [cigar smoking] is to friendship and Christian patience I have sometimes regretted that I never began to smoke."[31]

It's too late for Machen to experience first-hand what he called "his idea of delight," but maybe Michael Horton could realize this desire on Machen's behalf.

❧ Yet More Great Moments in ❧ Literature and Film if a Main Character Was Replaced by *Cigar Aficionado's* James Suckling

Rocky IV

Rocky "Suckling" Balboa, in the ring, after beating Ivan Drago on Christmas Eve and ending the Cold War. "If I can change . . . (pauses for translation) . . . and you's can change . . . EVERYBODY CAN CHANGE! And by change, I of course mean change the way you purchase and store your cigars. You people need to make sure the humidity in your cigar environment never gets above or below certain pre-determined levels." And all of the Russians in attendance stood up and cheered for their new hero.

Gone With the Wind

In his role as a rakish, devil-may-care blockade runner during the Civil War, Rhett Suckling—instead of providing the usual weaponry to various Confederate enclaves— instead throws lavish wine-and-cheese tastings (invitation only) for soldiers on both sides of the conflict. This results in a completely different level of dialogue and understanding between the two sides, and instead of a bloody, years-long war costing hundreds of thousands of American lives, the (incredibly civil) "Civil War" is re-branded as a wine event pitting Northern wines and Southern wines against one another, annually, and is sponsored by *Cigar Aficionado* which Rhett Suckling initially invests-in and the eventually owns-outright. He never meets Scarlett O'Hara whom he never gets an opportunity to give-or-not-give a damn about, because he's too busy managing the annual event and running the magazine.

Back to the Future

```
Marty McSuckling:   "Too loud." I can't believe it.
                    I'm never gonna get a chance to
                    play in front of anybody.

Jennifer Parker:    Marty, one rejection isn't the
                    end of the world.

Marty McSuckling:   I just don't think I'm cut out
                    for music. Rather, I think I'm
                    cut out for a life spent
                    walking along the tobacco
                    groves in Central America, sort
                    of "inspecting" the leaves in a
                    thoughtful way, and then also
                    tasting and collecting fine
                    aged wines...and doing the same
                    thing in the groves of
                    grapes...and by the same thing
                    I mean the walking along and
                    inspecting.

Jennifer Parker:    Oh.
```

Infinite Jest

Instead of sneaking to the basement catacombs of the Enfield Tennis Academy to smoke marijuana, young tennis prodigy Hal Sucklingdenza sneaks down there to smoke Romeo y Julietas. As a result he has no interest in the AA / Addiction-Recovery community in Boston, which lops about 600 pages off the novel, making it much easier to carry around but otherwise not changing the story a whole lot.

On Golden Pond

"Suckling, you old poop."

Humidors

Why take the time and expense of selecting the perfect cigars only to let them immediately begin deteriorating? Don't scrimp on the humidor, people. It's a place to store your cigars, a way to show your unique personality (if indeed you have a unique personality), and most importantly a device for preserving your investment.

I've met a number of casual cigar smokers who thought they didn't actually need a humidor. Here's the thing: if someone tells you that keeping your cigars in the refrigerator will do the trick, you can safely disregard everything he or she tells you about cigars (and probably everything else). This is likely the same person who told you to keep your coffee beans in the freezer. (He was wrong about that too.)

A good humidor is mostly air-tight, but allows just a little exchange to take place (i.e., don't set that heavy ashtray on your humidor lid.) The inside is almost invariably Spanish cedar, which is not from Spain and not actually cedar, but it does a nice job of maintaining humidity, it seasons your cigars nicely, and tobacco beetles *hate* it.

Along with your cigars, you will find two vital pieces of equipment inside a humidor: the regulator (the actual humidifying element) and the hygrometer (which measures the humidity, allowing you to make the appropriate adjustments). There are three main modes of humidification used in a standard humidor: some regulators take only distilled water (which needs to be replenished quite often), others use a propylene glycol solution, and some people swear by silica gel beads (warning: never add propylene glycol to your silica gel beads . . . they don't get along).

Hygrometers also come in different types, namely analog and digital. Most entry-level desktop humidors come with a crummy regulator and a plastic analog hygrometer. It's fine to buy one of these "starter" humidors, but be sure to upgrade these two elements, as properly calibrating a cheap plastic hygrometer is quite literally impossible, since it will immediately begin to drift and you will never know if your humidor is doing its job or not until you notice that your cigars are crunchy. Also, almost every digital hygrometer additionally contains a built-in digital thermometer, giving you all the information you need to maintain a cigar-friendly environment within the walls of that beautiful box.

Some very expensive humidors will have an "active regulation system," meaning they continually monitor and adjust the humidity for you, but these are found almost exclusively in walk-ins and large cabinet humidors and it's plenty easy (and a little fun for obsessive people like myself) to check in on your cigars regularly and keep everything where it needs to be. Remember the 70/70 rule. That's your goal: 70% relative humidity and 70° F. It's fine to go a little in either direction with both, but never let your humidor get warmer than 77 degrees, as tobacco beetles can hatch in such an environment.

Your humidor will come with instructions on how to properly season and maintain it. Follow these to the letter. Your manly instinct to toss the manual and figure it out for yourself will not help you in this case. Keep everything as it should be and you won't have to stress over cigars "going bad," freeing you to buy a box at a time even if you're a more occasional smoker. Remember, the aging of cigars is vital so that the different elements of the filler can blend together. This has already been done to a fine cigar before it was shipped to the store, but there's no reason you shouldn't age them further. If kept in a humidor in the right conditions, ten years is not too long a period for a fine cigar to age.

There are five basic classes of humidors, as follows:

Travel humidor—Also called "pocket humidors," these range in size to accommodate one to ten cigars and are designed for temporary use when travelling. You don't need a travel humidor when you bring three cigars to the golf course (a disposable plastic zipper bag will do just fine), but if you're bringing cigars on a weekend trip, it may be worthwhile to invest in one of these.

Desktop humidor - This is what most cigar smokers use to store their stash and it meets their needs just fine. You can fit 25-80 cigars in an average personal humidor (depending on the size, duh). They range in quality and aesthetic from exotic and very expensive to plain (or plain ugly) and cheap.

Table humidor - These are larger, fancier pieces, often featuring a window in the top so you can look at the hundreds of cigars housed within, without letting the humidity out. The outside generally features fine polished stone or wood with inlays.

Cabinet humidor - This is a piece of furniture, not a desktop accessory. It can hold literally thousands of cigars. You probably do a lot of entertaining if you have/need one of these and you probably have more friends than you would if you didn't have one.

Walk-in humidor - If you own a walk-in, it's probably next to your wine cellar and adjacent to the hook where you stow the keys to your Learjet. Enjoy it, moneybags! Of course, I'm just being nasty because I'm jealous. Many people with no jet at all have built walk-in humidors in their basements (or walk-in humidor-slash-wine cellar combinations, splitting the difference between the desired relative humidities). If you can make a walk-in humidor happen in your home, Gut Check salutes you. Really. E-mail us a picture of your humidor and we'll e-mail you back a picture of us, holding today's newspaper, saluting you.

Can dried-out cigars be revived?

Yes, they can with proper love and care and *time* in your humidor. Don't jack up the humidity to try and make up for the neglect; just put them in the regular 70/70 and *forget about them* for a while. It will take longer to bring them back than it took them to dry out.

Did You Just Say "Tobacco Beetles?"

Why, yes, we did. A couple times.

If your cigar has a little "vent" that is spewing a tiny stream of smoke, you've probably got a beetle situation on your hands. If you just bought the cigar at a cigar lounge, return it. Any tobacconist worth his salt will replace a beetled smoke with a fresh one.

If the cigar came out of your own humidor, then you need to take action, and quick. The way to kill these horrible little reminders of the Fall is to put your cigars, in small bundles, into little paper bags, which you then put in freezer-safe plastic zipper bags (not a no-name brand). You then place *that* in a larger plastic zipper bag, then freeze them for a full week, just to be sure. Then move the bag into the fridge (preferably in a humidity-controlled vegetable crisper). When they have thawed, place them back in your humidor.

But wait—are you smoking *dead beetles* now?! Well, yeah, but you're smoking their eggs like 90% of the time anyway. And, if the urban legends are to be believed, there are moth eggs in your Frosted Flakes. Just try not to think about it.

G.K. CHESTERTON

Chesterton is perhaps the most widely quoted man in the church today. Those sermon illustration collections that seem to multiply in pastors' studies are chock full of the witty, cutting, and dead-on observations and musings of this incredibly gifted author, who almost always had a cigar pinched between his lips (and also enjoyed his pipe). He is so frequently quoted in evangelical sermons and books today that many Protestants may not know he was Roman Catholic. But he was, as is clear from this quintessentially Chestertonian quote:

"The Catholic Church is like a thick steak, a glass of red wine, and a good cigar."

-G.K. Chesterton

Every Cigar Smoker's Essential Guide to Living with His Wife

by Erin Bartels, wife of a cigar smoker

Men! Despite the fact that this is written by a woman, don't skip to the next "More Great Moments in Literature and Film if a Main Character Was Replaced by Cigar Aficionado's James Suckling." Trust me, it will be worth your time. Why? Because nothing ruins a good smoke like an angry wife. You want to keep that woman in your life happy.

There are four basic kinds of wives of cigar smokers:

- the verbal, angry wife
- the silent, angry wife
- the rule-setting wife
- the cigar-smoking wife

Different factors will push a woman into one category or another. Timing is a big one. If you took up smoking sometime *after* your wedding, for instance, you many find yourself dealing with an angry wife (silent or verbal). Your father-in-law is another. Does he smoke? Does he disapprove? Did he die of lung cancer? Her relationship with him will affect your relationship with her.

So which category does your wife fall under? And, more importantly, how can you move her into a more desirable, less-naggy category? Let's break it down, shall we?

Verbal, Angry Wife (VAW)

The VAW is the wife who doesn't like cigar smoke and takes every opportunity to tell you so. She might be passive aggressive about it or (admittedly more rare) aggressive-aggressive about it. She might tell you your clothes stink, your hair stinks, your breath stinks. She might cite a litany of smoking related ailments worthy of the Surgeon General. She might accuse you of purposefully ruining her life. She might even snatch a lit cigar from between your stunned teeth and put it out on your forehead. The VAW is not to be trifled with. Frankly, if you can't persuade her to jump categories, you might better off quitting the cigars. Remember Proverbs 21:9 (also 21:19 and 25:24).

Silent, Angry Wife (SAW)

The SAW is the wife who doesn't like cigar smoke but also doesn't like direct confrontation. Rather than say something outright about your smoking habit, she will leave brochures about lung cancer and emphysema scattered about the house. She might collect all of your matches and lighters and "accidentally" throw them away. She probably sighs a lot and mock coughs every time you come in from having a smoke out on the deck. It's possible to live in relative peace with an SAW as long as you consistently buy her flowers, get your dirty clothes in the hamper, use mouthwash and a tongue-scraper, and never expect sex the same day you smoke a cigar.

Rule-Setting Wife (RSW)

The RSW is the wife who doesn't mind if you smoke, but has some rules about the whole enterprise. She is generally indifferent to smoking, seeing it as neither sinful nor disgusting, but insists that you only smoke in certain places, possibly at certain times, and only around certain people. She may allow you the deck, your car (as long as she doesn't have to drive it or ride in it), and/or the garage (by the driveway, not the door to the mudroom). She may limit smoking to when you walk the dog or only after the kids have gone to bed. Her list of people not to smoke in front of may include your pastor's wife, anyone associated with your kid's school, her mother, and any and all children. The RSW is a good wife. She's just trying to keep your house nice and your image clean. Cut her a break.

Cigar-Smoking Wife (CSW)

The CSW is the wife who not only couldn't care a fig about whether you smoke—they're your lungs, after all—she will occasionally enjoy a fine cigar right alongside you. She'll probably buy you cigars for your birthday or Father's Day. When she sees lighters on sale or has a chance to bring home some free matches from a wedding reception, she'll hoard as many as possible so that you never find yourself with a great cigar between your teeth but nothing with which to light it. She won't freak out if your son puts a straw in his mouth and says it's a cigar. She understands how relaxing a cigar is, how conducive to gentile conversation, how essential a component of watching a boxing match on pay-per-view. The CSW is the ideal wife for the cigar smoker.

If you've just read these categories and find that you are yoked to a VAW, you have my sympathies. It's a rough road, but it's not necessarily a dead end. With time and patience (and doing everything in your power not to antagonize her) she may someday turn into an SAW or even an RSW. Try to think of something she does that drives you crazy and let it go. Perhaps when she sees you make a move toward harmony and liberty, she'll feel the need to return that grace. The same tactic can bring an SAW to RSW status.

If your wife is already an RSW, you should probably count your blessings and leave well enough alone. Sure, it sucks to be banished to the out-of-doors during a harsh Midwestern winter, but even then you'll find that those friends of yours with the VAWs and SAWs are happy to huddle next to a space heater in your open garage and smoke a cigar in peace. And a word of advice: invite your lovely wife to join you sometime. The more she smells that delicious smoke the more likely she'll be to light one up herself. Maybe—just maybe—she'll make the leap to CSW.

And if you are one of the happy few who live with a CSW, congratulations. I have no advice to give save this: tell her you brag about her to the other guys whose wives give them such a hard time for smoking. She'll walk a little taller just knowing that.

Erin Bartels is a copywriter by day, a novelist by night, and spent much of 2013 writing one short story each month. She blogs regularly about writing, nature, photography, and more at **www.erinbartels.com** and lives with her husband and their son in Lansing, Michigan, somewhere between angry protesters on the Capitol lawn and raucous frat boys at nearby Michigan State University.

CHARLES COLSON

Chuck Colson didn't get the best start, what with his involvement in Watergate and all that, but only the jerkiest jerks had anything but kind words to say when the man died. In addition to all sorts of ministry (primarily to prisoners), Colson wrote many incredible books, hosted a radio program, and helped us relate our faith to the world around us. Most of us can picture several famous pictures of Colson clutching his beloved pipe, but were you aware that, in his office in Virginia,Colson kept one of C.S. Lewis' pipes in a glass case? You are now awesomer for knowing that. You're welcome.

LIGHTING YOUR CIGARS

People hold oddly-passionate views on how one should light a cigar. Ultimately, some methods are better than others, but only a couple of them are full-on unforgiveable.

Let's start with the obvious: there's a reason the tobacconist puts a box of matches in the bag with every purchase of fine cigars. Use them. The wood of a long match will season the first few puffs of your cigar, but in a pleasant way.

Remember George Bluth, Sr. describing how to light a cigar properly to Hell Boy? Take his advice to heart. But never try to light a cigar with paper matches from a book—you'd be better off using the stove burner like Rocco after he got his finger shot off.

If you must use a lighter, remember why you're a cigar smoker to begin with and avoid dumpy-looking, plasticky, or domestic-beer-themed lighters, as these make the world a sadder place. Ironically, though, be aware that a liquid fuel lighter (like that monogrammed Zippo your best man gave you) is going to leave its chemically mark on the flavor of your cigar—at least for the first few puffs—while a standard plastic butane Bic will not. What a conundrum.

Not to worry—you can certainly light up in style *without* compromising taste. There are plenty of high quality, cigar-friendly lighters out there. In fact, many fine cigar manufacturers sell their own lighters (or include them in multi-packs of their cigars). The two basic groups of cigar-friendly lighters are **standard flame** and **torch**.

Torches work better in my book (although I avoid the ones with the translucent reservoir of fuel that look like they should be boiling something illegal in a blackened spoon). Torch lighters are my preference because I feel like I have more control when lighting, but many experienced smokers see them as an abomination. Other purists insist on lighting their cigars with cedar strips. Still others (e.g., James Suckling, Joel Osteen, and, surprisingly, Dave Ramsey) think that a burning hundred dollar bill is conducive to an even light and adds a little "hint of Ben Franklin" to the flavor.

Whatever implement you use, the technique is just as important. If you're burning the wrapper black, you're doing it wrong. Here's the proper method: try to evenly toast the foot of the cigar without it actually touching the flame, almost like cauterizing a wound (why did my mind go *there*?). Your cigar will almost certainly touch the flame, but that's okay. Roll the cigar over the flame for a moment, sparingly and *evenly*, until you've got a decently uniform toasting going. You don't want to be able to see the sharp ends of tobacco leaf filler.

Don't rush this; an uneven initial lighting will make the whole cigar an asymmetrical, frustrating experience as you continually try to fix a problem that grows with every puff. A good practice at this point is to blow gently on the now-burning foot of the cigar to even out any problem areas. Now, put the cigar in your mouth (not the burning end!) and slowly turn it over the flame while drawing on it lightly. Make one full rotation and you should be set. Practice makes perfect.

What about re-lighting?

There are a couple reasons you might find yourself needing to re-light. First of all, if despite your efforts, you find your cigar burning down at an extreme angle, you may reach the point where you just want to cut your losses, clip the end straight, and re-light. (This is when a sharp pair of scissor cutters will come in handy.) After cutting, puff *out* a couple times to expel any smoke inside the cigar and wait a few minutes to let it cool before you re-light (unless you like the bitter taste of tar).

The other reason to re-light is if you smoke part of a cigar and then need to abandon it before you've finished (but you can't stand the thought of the remainder going to waste). Let me tell you what *not* to do in this case: don't do what I did a couple years ago when I had just sat down on the front porch to enjoy a cigar and my wife pulled into the driveway with groceries. I quickly clipped the end and set it aside and (because I'm a gentleman) brought in all the heavy stuff. Now, here's what my stupid brain said to itself: "You only took two puffs and you removed the burned part and the cigar is cool; why not put it back in the humidor to smoke tomorrow?" Then my stupid brain answered, "Great idea," and did just that.

Humidor ruined.

The Spanish cedar soaked up all the stink of the partially smoked cigar and transferred it to all of its little friends. If saving cigars to relight later is your thing, invest in a Cigar Saver (there are several different kinds out there that work in slightly different ways) so you can keep the veteran away from the sweet, untouched reserves. And, again, remember to *puff out* all the old smoke before you stash it, and make sure you re-light and finish the cigar within a day or two.

What's That White Stuff?

Perhaps you've noticed a dusting of white powder on a cigar you've just purchased or one you've been storing. Your initial fear might be that this is mold and that the cigar is ruined. Don't worry; if yor cigar is moldy, there will be a definite green color to it. So what's this powder? Well, if you're a very powerful man with diabolical enemies, it may be Anthrax, I suppose. But more likely, this is just what we refer to as "bloom" or "plume," a normal byproduct of properly aging. Go ahead and wipe it off before you smoke to the glory of God.

FATHER DAMIEN

Lest we unintentionally promote the myth that only the rich, powerful, and stuffy enjoy the gentle art of smoking (via our hall of academics, theologians, popes, poets, etc.), let us remember St. Damien of Molokai, the priest who chose to give his life ministering to people in Hawaii. What's that? Doesn't sound like much of a sacrifice? Did we mention the people to whom he ministered were lepers? Day after day, Father Damien told the scum of the earth, "Jesus loves you lepers," until the day that he stood before them and told them, "Jesus loves us lepers," having contracted the disease himself. Father Damien smoked a pipe to try and cover over the stench of the leprosy all around him. It was also a keen reminder (as it was for Bonhoeffer) that, even in the midst of suffering and pain, God continues to cause his sun to shine, his rain to fall, and showers us with good things to enjoy and for which to return thanks.

20 WAYS TO SMOKE CIGARS TO THE GLORY OF GOD

by Jared Wilson

As an occasional cigar smoker for going on 14 years (I started before it became a fad and kept going after the fad waned), I have some thoughts on how one might partake of cigars to the glory of God. Here are 20 of them:

1. Smoke slowly and reflectively, as part of the discipline of contemplation on God's Word.

2. Most cigar smokers I know look at their cigar a lot while they are smoking, up close, tracing with their gaze the veins in the leaves and admiring the burnish of the oils in the wrapper. A good cigar is a work of art. It makes me happy and makes me thank God for his good creation.

3. Smoke outside and thank God for the skies and the clouds and the grass and the trees.

4. My college religion professor, the late great Princeton-trained M.B. Jackson, used to exit the classroom during test time, pipe in hand, saying, "If you need me, I'll be on the steps sending up a burnt offering." That's a good notion. Cigar smokers like the look of the smoke. Think of it as a burnt offering of thanks to the Maker of all good things.

5. The smoldering tip of the cigar is both enticing and dangerous. Like the sin that leads to hell. There's an illustration for you cigar smoking preachers out there.

6. The proper storage of good cigars takes regular monitoring and care (humidification, temperature,

etc.). Mindfulness and intentionality are virtues lacking in the modern Church, and we can thank God that taking care of cigars helps cure "hurry sickness."

7. Good tobacco is cultivated, cured, and rolled by hard working men and women in parts of the world most of us will never visit. I think about this every time I smoke a cigar, what calloused, hard-working, talented hands created my cigar. Pray for those people, that God would grant them long life and health and happiness, and thank God for them and their giftedness.

8. Thank God that he makes places in the world specifically conditioned to produce perfect tobacco: the right climate, the right soil, the right farmers. There are no coincidences.

9. Don't inhale cigar smoke into your lungs.

10. Add your ashes to compost or dump them into the grass or flower beds, as a good steward of creation.

11. Have a Bible study or theological discussion group at a cigar lounge.

12. Hang out where people you don't know smoke cigars and build conversational bridges that allow you to be a witness to the gospel.

13. Smoke with good Christian friends, laughing a lot and talking about things that matter (and don't), and thank God for fellowship. As someone who does this regularly, I can say there is almost nothing more comforting to my soul than smoking stogies long into the night and just enjoying the camaraderie of good Christian friendship.

14. Give good cigars—good ones!—out as gifts on more occasions than just the birth of a child.

15. Marvel that someone along the way figured out how to turn the tobacco plant into a cigar (or pipe tobacco) and see that human ingenuity and creativity is a result of being made in the image of God.

16. For the married smokers, thank God you have an awesome wife who is cool with you smoking. (This assumes you have an awesome wife who is cool with you smoking. If you don't, thank God you have a wife who cares about your health, your reputation, your good breath, or whatever the grounds are for her disapproval.)

17. As you smoke, think of all the famous cigar smokers you can—comedians and writers and actors and painters and poets and filmmakers—and thank God for their artistry (and for art in general).

18. Pick a spot in your Bible. Light your cigar. Start reading and don't stop until you're smoking a nub. Beats using an hourglass or timer.

19. Take two outside. Light one up. Wait for your neighbor to come outside, then offer him the other.

20. If you buy in bulk, turn the empty boxes into care packages for soldiers or children in third world countries.

Originally published in 2008. Reprinted with permission.

JARED C. WILSON

Jared Wilson is the pastor of Middletown Springs Community Church in Middletown Springs, Vermont and the author of several books, including *Your Jesus Is Too Safe*, *Gospel Wakefulness*, and *The Pastor's Justification*. You can find his blog on www.thegospelcoalition.org and connect with Jared at www.jaredcwilson.com.

"Thank God that he makes places in the world specifically conditioned to produce perfect tobacco: the right climate, the right soil, the right farmers. There are no coincidences."

99

Cigars in Ministry Timeline

As any given afternoon in Timothy's Fine Cigars will confirm, many pastors love to smoke cigars and pipes. This affinity doesn't come out of nowhere, and usually follows a particular arc, as follows:

Bible College

So you're in Bible college, which means that you're nineteen and full of vigor, but the majority of the excitement in your life comes from "breaking curfew" or indulging in activities that might get you kicked out of Bible college. To that end, you and your friends regularly (read: maybe twice a semester) smoke cigars. You don't know much about them, but you've grown accustomed to those things with the Spanish name in the glass tube, purchased at a high-end (well, kind of high-end) gas station. You save all the bands and the tubes as a reminder of your edginess (much like real college students saving all their import beer bottles). In the mirror of your mind, you are Mark Driscoll, pushing the envelope, but not in a full-on rebellious way.

Seminary

You're broke, but you still want to project an image of refinement and cement your place as a full-fledged member of the intelligentsia, who would never smoke something that came in a glass tube or from a gas station. You own a pipe and like the idea of smoking it, but you have a hard time keeping it lit, so cigars remain your preferred smoke. You tell yourself you're an Ashton man, but more often than not, you buy cigars in a four-pack from the wine store down the street (which is really a liquor store). Everyone else at your seminary also secretly does this, but it makes you feel like you're the one guy there who won't wind up some day wearing a translucent short-sleeved button up shirt with pit-stains over a wife beater (visible through the dress shirt) and tie that reaches only to your belly button. You see yourself, of course, as a young Charles Spurgeon or, occasionally (when you smoke your pipe) as Lewis without the penchant for paganism.

Youth Pastor

Officially, you don't smoke cigars, but you're ever on the look-out for the "Cool Dad" in your church in whom you can confide your secret love of stogies. Cool Dad will then invite you over for steaks on the grill and after-dinner fine cigars to be enjoyed amidst theological conversation. But you never find him because he doesn't exist. You think of yourself as the Brad Pitt character in a movie about youth ministry—if such a thing existed.

College Pastor

You're a college pastor. You've outgrown the Jesus fish tattoo on your ankle. Your acoustic guitar just sits in the corner of your office, fondly recounting the days of being playfully strummed under a tree by a shirtless you. Of course, you can't sit shirtless under a tree and strum a guitar anymore because it's inappropriate to make the female college students under your charge swoon. And because you're developing man-boobs.

In addition to booking chapel speakers and overseeing the Internet Integrity program on campus, you occasionally find time to fire up a clove cigarette or cheap cigar you bought in a bundle on the Internet seven years ago (but not on the campus network, because the filters you installed would have blocked it). You sit all alone behind your privacy fence and smoke with a steady stream of air freshener and a battery powered fan, because, while you intentionally drafted the "Life Together Covenant" with a loophole for cigars, you're always afraid someone will find and fill said loophole. You see yourself as Karl Barth, whom you haven't really read.

Hipster Pastor

You started smoking cigars about the same time you planted your church, but soon realized it was just too mainstream (much like church planting). So you moved on to pipes and then realized that all your seminary classmates also smoked pipes. Then you moved on to Lucky Strikes, which you pretended to like for a couple weeks, but not enough people got the irony.

As of now, you enjoy an occasional stop at the local hookah bar, but mostly you're finding bits of tree bark and grass clippings on your lawn and rolling them in paper from your recycle bin, because it's the most ecological way to smoke and because no one else is doing it yet. You see yourself as a cooler version of You.

Associate Pastor

In between planning and selecting small group resources and ... well, no one's sure what else you do, you have plenty of time to smoke the "Cuban cigars" that one of your congregants picked up for you at the airport on the way back from Sandals. They never taste as good as you hoped. You see yourself as Charles Spurgeon's associate pastor.

Senior Pastor

For the first few years of your ministry, you enjoyed a relaxing smoke once a week, which blossomed into a "cigar lounge Bible study." But after preaching a particularly self-convicting sermon about the weaker brother you've never actually met, you decided to "take a break." Your humidor has been bone dry for nigh on a decade, but you still think of yourself as a cigar connoisseur-slash-Charles Spurgeon.

Megachurch Pastor

You really felt called to that six-figure salary, the $15,000 espresso machine in the lobby, and the "company car," which happens to be a Mercedes Benz (although it's three years old, *ahem*). When you finish writing your talk for the week, you hit the golf course for "staff meeting" where you enjoy a Cohiba with thirty-seven your associate pastors, all of whom are smoking a lesser cigar but only about three or four of whom actually enjoy cigars (or golf). The rest of them are all battling over the Big Promotion at work, which, oddly, is also church. You see yourself as the Gordon Gekko character from *Wall Street* if that character wasn't completely evil, and was also a Christian, and was also a pastor.

MORE GREAT MOMENTS IN LITERATURE AND FILM IF A MAIN CHARACTER WAS REPLACED BY *CIGAR AFICIONADO'S* JAMES SUCKLING

Romeo and Juliet

Juliet: "Romeo, O Romeo, wherefore art thou, Romeo?"

Romeo (Suckling): "I'm actually sipping an aged Chablis, while enjoying a 2009 Davidoff with hints of flint and chestnut on the finish. Why, where are you?"

Jerry Maguire

Dorothy "Suckling" Boyd: "You complete me," in reference not to Jerry Maguire, but to an exquisite bottle of dry red wine.

Braveheart

William "Suckling" Wallace: "All men die, but only a few really live . . . and of course, for me, truly living means a country estate, a humidor full of premium cigars, and a cask of fine cognac. They can take our lives, but they can't take our tobacco products!" At which point, Suckling's soldiers look at him quizzically and, instead of racing down into battle, just sort of walk off aimlessly. At which point (again), Suckling produces a bottle of wine, a cigar, and a small plate of prosciutto and shaved parmesan cheese, not wanting to waste a good verdant, hillside picnic.

Dead Poets Society

English teacher John Suckling inspires his students to a love of poetry and to seize the day. "The Day" being a limited edition label for a buttery Napa Valley Chardonnay.

OTHER PLACES TO SMOKE

If the weather's nice and you'd rather not spend an hour in a dark, semi-depressing cigar store environment, there are a number of places to smoke. We've broken down a few locations below, and listed the pros and cons of each.

Inside Your House.

Advantages: This is the Holy Grail of cigar smoking locations. Your ability to smoke inside means that you are one of the following: a.) single, b.) married to a cigar-smoking wife (the Holy Grail of wives), or c.) making a huge mistake.

Disadvantages: That fan that you put in the window isn't going to do the job. It will smell like one big ashtray in here tomorrow, and how are you going to explain that? Also, that "Smoke Erase" spray you bought at the tobacco shop is just going to make the place smell like cigar-scented lilacs.

On the Deck

Advantages: This is a much more realistic and wife-friendly locale in which to smoke. On a perfect day—70 and sunny with a slight breeze, no mosquitoes, no rain, no kids running in and out—the deck smoke rivals the finest cigar lounge.

Disadvantages: The day I described above only happens about three times a year.

In Your Garage

Advantages: This is where you smoke if it's raining on the deck. The garage is dry, and you won't get rained on in there. Also, there's an abundance of folding chairs (and, probably, a couple of cars).

Disadvantages: Although you've made a halfhearted attempt to turn your garage into a "cigar lounge" (meaning you have a kerosene heater in the middle of the folding chairs, and also a vintage beer sign on the wall), it's not really working. Unless your garage doubles as the set of *The Godfather*, it probably lacks a certain classy, oak-paneled ethos and is instead a place where your kids keep their bikes and skateboards, and you keep your lawnmower and weed-whip, which automatically makes it one of the most depressing places on earth. And if you're in the garage avoiding the rain, chances are the mosquitoes are doing the same thing.

In Your Car

Disadvantages: You tell yourself that you'll keep the window open and the air moving through; however, if the air is moving through it also means that it's blowing the ash all over your clothes, upholstery, and skin. Your cigar begins to unravel, and you realize that if you're driving over 15 miles per hour, it's impossible to enjoy a cigar in your car.

Advantages: None.

Walking Around Downtown

Advantages: You feel like a high roller, walking around all the tall buildings and stuff, and it makes you wistful for the days when you could actually enjoy a cigar while eating in a classy restaurant.

Disadvantages: Other people. Unless it's 1960, you're Don Draper, and everyone else in town was magically transported there from the set of *Mad Men*, chances are good that That One Lady will follow you around and cough (subtext: she's annoyed by your cigar). Her presence will ruin your cigar and also your day. Not that this has happened to us.

Around a Campfire

Advantages: It's a way for Indoorsmen to redeem camping, and it's pretty much the only place in America that hasn't gone "Smoke Free!" No one can complain around a campfire because there's already smoke in their eyes.

Disadvantages: This means that you're camping.

Smoking with Patience

Always bear in mind that cigars and pipes are to be enjoyed in an unhurried fashion. That poor sap squeezing three quarters of a cigarette into the two minutes between memorial service and funeral procession is an addict and, as such, is not enjoying what he is doing. You are the very opposite of him in the way you enjoy your cigar and / or pipe. Drawing on either with too much gusto or too frequently can cause a bitter taste, heat the cigar (or pipe) to an uncomfortable level, and ruining the aesthetic. Instead, wait at least thirty seconds between draws to let the cigar cool. Don't worry that you're "wasting" what little smoke floats off the end while the cigar rests; you're not wasting it any more than you're wasting the smell of steak wafting up off your eighteen dollar New York Strip.

If there's a theme running through this little book, it's that smoking a cigar or pipe should be a protected period of time for fellowship, reflection, prayer, reading, enjoying nature, meditation on Scripture, etc. When you start toking on the end of your cigar as if you were on some sort of five minute "smoke break," you've missed the whole point. However, if you do get overeager and find your cigar heating up, do the following: draw in very lightly for a few seconds and then puff out several times to expel the hot smoke. Let the cigar rest for a minute or two, and resume.

As you smoke, resist the urge to continually tap at the ashtray to knock off the ash as it appears. We've been programmed by the cigarette smokers around us (with the exception of that one grizzled old chain-smoking woman on your street growing up, whose cigarette ash was always an inch long) to compulsively flick and tap at smoking materials as if the ash were an embarrassment. Once again, these are the worst possible role models when it comes to enjoying a fine smoke. It is a mark of a fine long-fill cigar that its ash will grow incredibly long. For that reason, let it grow. Enjoy watching the tightly bunched cinders cool and turn gray while keeping their form. Anticipate the next puff.

Let me tell you a story: when I signed my first book deal, Ted and I had our first thirty-dollar Davidoffs by way of a celebratory *we-would-never-do-this-in-real-life*[32] type of activity and decided to see just how long the ash would get on these heavenly smokes if we left it alone and let it grow. We wussed out and reset the smokes when we began to worry about smoldering clothes, but there's no reason to think it couldn't have gone well beyond the three-inch ash these cigars achieved. When you fear your ash is in danger of falling, don't tap it—rather, *roll* the ash firmly-but-gently against the inside of the ash tray. Tapping can lead to a "pointy" cigar, which can cause blockages and keep you from experiencing the blend the way the cigar's maker intended. Waiting and rolling will ensure an even smoke.

So, how far down should you smoke a fine cigar? There are people who tell you to stop when you hit the halfway point. In my opinion, these people are either 1. crazy, 2. ill-informed, or 3. incredibly rich. (Check and see if they wash and reuse their bath towels or simply throw them away and buy more.)

Granted, if you're smoking an inferior product, it won't mature well (i.e. the taste will get worse, not better, as you go) and it may turn on you half-way through. In this case, yes, go ahead and stop...*smoking those crummy cigars.* Can you see how it makes more sense to pay $15 for one good cigar, rather than $6 a piece for two mediocre half-cigars?

As to where exactly one should stop, that's up to individual taste. Ted tends to call it quits with about a third of the cigar left (if Gut

I'm with the Band

If you are going to remove the band, wait until the burning end of the cigar gets close to it. The heat will soften the glue and you won't rip the cigar's wrapper.

Check's picking up the tab) or with a quarter or less remaining (if he bought the thing out-of-pocket). Zach tends to smoke a really good cigar right down to the nub. You've probably been in a cigar lounge or two where people used toothpicks (sort of redneck) or some kind of clamp or clip (pretty ghetto) when the cigar has gotten too small to hold, and hopefully what you've seen has sufficiently turned you off to that concept.

Just remember, the point of a cigar is enjoyment and, at whatever point your enjoyment begins to wane, put it down before the last few puffs tarnish all that came before. Notice I said "put it down," not "put it out." When you've finished a cigar, the proper thing to do is simply set it down in the ash tray. You're a gentleman smoking a cigar, after all, not a hit man mashing out a cigarette butt before whacking a "canary" who was about to "sing." Anyway, you might think actively extinguishing a cigar will save the people around you breathing unnecessary smoke, but the fact is that snuffing it out creates a foul and unnecessary odor.

❦ YET MORE GREAT MOMENTS IN ❧ LITERATURE AND FILM IF A MAIN CHARACTER WAS REPLACED BY *CIGAR AFICIONADO'S* JAMES SUCKLING

Little House on the Prairie

Pa "Suckling" Ingalls, instead of tilling the land and planting corn and shoeing the horses and repairing that hole in the side of the barn, decides to spend the season tasting different cigar wrappers, shades, and blends and while the family really enjoys his aesthetic discovery, a hard winter later hits the prairie and they all die of consumption.

The Bourne Identity

Instead of using his government-infused superpowers to hunt down the people who stole his identity, Jason Suckling uses said powers to rob a chain of high-end wineries in California's Napa Valley.

"I can tell you the license plate numbers of all six cars outside. I can tell you that our waitress is left-handed that I can smoke three full-bodied cigars in a row before my hands start shaking. Now why would I know that? How can I know that and not know who I am?"

Lord of the Flies

Suckling Piggy, as the island's true cognoscente, wins the loyalty of all the stranded boys when he perfects his Island Wine and manages a small but productive tobacco plant-ation, producing a bumper crop and keeping them all in cigars and drink. When given a chance to leave the island, they all refuse, explaining, "We've never lived so well."

Cigar & Pipe Hall of Fame

Johann Sebastian Bach

Bach is best known for writing *Ode to Joy,* which is, in turn, best known for being the score to one of the *Die Hard* movies. Wait, no—that was that filthy *Beethoven.* By contrast, Bach seems to have been a genuine believer who loved his Savior and strove to glorify him with all the music he created. He also wrote verse, including the following spiritual look at smoking his pipe:

Whene'er I take my pipe and stuff it

And smoke to pass the time away
My thoughts, as I sit there and puff it,
Dwell on a picture sad and grey:
It teaches me that very like
Am I myself unto my pipe.

Like me this pipe, so fragrant burning,
Is made of naught but earthen clay;
To earth I too shall be returning,
And cannot halt my slow decay.
My well used pipe, now cracked and broken,
Of mortal life is but a token.

No stain, the pipe's hue yet doth darken;
It remains white. Thus do I know
That when to death's call I must harken
My body, too, all pale will grow.
To black beneath the sod 'twill turn,
Likewise the pipe, if oft it burn.

Or when the pipe is fairly glowing,
Behold then instantaneously,
The smoke off into thin air going,
'Til naught but ash is left to see.
Man's fame likewise away will burn
And unto dust his body turn.

How oft it happens when one's smoking,
The tamper's missing from its shelf,
And one goes with one's finger poking
Into the bowl and burns oneself.
If in the pipe such pain doth dwell
How hot must be the pains of Hell!

Thus o'er my pipe in contemplation
Of such things—I can constantly
Indulge in fruitful meditation,
And so, puffing contentedly,
On land, at sea, at home, abroad,
I smoke my pipe and worship God.

"I believe that many who find that 'nothing happens' when they sit down, or kneel down, to a book of devotion, would find that the heart sings unbidden while they are working their way through a tough bit of theology with a pipe in their teeth and a pencil in their hand.

—C.S. Lewis

in his preface to St. Athanasius's *On the Incarnation*

Appendix:
Suggested Hate Mail Templates

Dear Reader,

We know that sometimes we write things that either you don't like the style of, or that just flat-out make you angry. We know that sometimes you can take that emotion (anger) and stomp around your house in a fit of ranting, emotional energy, letting your significant other know all the ways that those guys from Gut Check are big jerks, and telling her that you're going to write a "strongly worded letter" that will just give those jerks "a piece of your mind."

The Internet has made this much easier, of course, given that you can vent your proverbial spleen all over Amazon.com via the one-star review, or you can leave a spleen-venting comment at one of our blogs. We know that raging out in this fashion is a part of the book business in the sort of postmodern, comment-on-everything culture we live in, but it's still a tremendous waste of your time and, let's be honest, ours too.

So we've gone ahead and saved you the trouble. Below are several hate mail templates which you can just print off and mail (like you're actually going to do that) or (more likely), copy and paste onto one of our blogs. We've put our collected publishing experience and intuition to work on what we feel like, humbly, are some truly exceptional pieces of anonymous hate mail. Anonymous, of course, because writers of messages like these never want to be known as the sort of people who write messages like these which creates, in you, a real serious internal conflict inasmuch as you want to say the nasty things but don't want to be the kind of guy that says the nasty things so as a sort of internal compromise you go ahead and write the nasty things but then figure that by not signing your name it's as though, in a sense (again), you never said-slash-wrote the things at all and also "anonymous" because you really don't want to go through the repercussions that may come with actually, courageously standing behind your opinions.

Rather than have you go through all that internal conflict we've just done the writing for you, and have even broken the missives down into categories. The anonymous posting is up to you.

Yours,
The Gut Check Team

PS: We know and respect the fact that some of you have real, conscience-level objections to smoking and we're not making light of that. We acknowledge and allow that there is freedom in Christ in these areas, but also acknowledge and respect differences of opinion / conviction (and we'd really love it if you could acknowledge/allow/respect in kind).

1. I'm Okay With You Guys But Hate Smoking

Dear Ted and Zach,

How can you guys do this? How can you encourage people to wantonly disregard their lung tissue and arterial integrity in this fashion? I mean, granted, you're not encouraging anyone to excessively smoke (or to smoke at all if they don't already), and you guys only smoke a couple cigars a month, and it's not like that's any more dangerous than eating a diet which is heavy in red meat or drinking lots of pop (and which I also, probably do). And I mean it's not like you're lighting cigars and placing them between the lips of the infirm or babies or kittens (which, the kittens, would admittedly be a really funny photo-graph)...

So my point is...umm...okay, never mind.

Regards,
Anonymous

2. I'm Allergic to Smoke and Am Overly Sensitive About It

Dear Ted and Zach,

You guys disgust me. How can you think it's okay to have your little quote/unquote gatherings which are exclusive and hurtful toward people like me who are allergic to smoke of any kind—so much so that even crackling campfires and autumn leaves burning and other idyllic fire scenarios leave me left out in the proverbial cold? I bet you also serve gluten and peanut products at these gatherings, which also disgusts and hurts me.

Hack Hack (that's a cough, affected to let you know how disgusting your little "gatherings" are).

- Anonymous

3. I'm a Hipster So I'm Totally Good With Cigars But Just Hate Your Theology and Some of Your Other Books and Am Taking This Opportunity to Tell You About It

Dear Ted and Zach,

I really love cigars and as much as I begrudgingly hate to say it, I also loved this book—especially the parts where you replaced certain movie characters with James Suckling. That was absolutely genius and broad and hipster and I wish I'd thought of it.

I'm actually writing to tell you how much offense I took to the books *Why We're Not Emergent and Kinda Christianity*. Even though I drive a Volvo, wear Toms, am sipping a microbrew while I type this on my affected retro typewriter purchased at Urban Outfitters, voted for Obama, am vague on gay marriage, and go to a worship gathering that meets at an abandoned factory that is so under-the-radar and hipster that it's not even abandoned yet (read: it's oper-

119

ational and we sort of meet between the whirring machines); I took offense at the way you broadly stereotyped.

I think you are full of yourselves and your literary style. I think you should step out of the way and let the gospel do the talking, and by the gospel I of course mean my particular set of experiences and affinities.

Signed,
Anonymous

4. The 10 millionth person to take I Corinthians 6:19 out of context wins a timeshare.

Dear Ted and Zach,

Don't you know that St. Paul called the body the temple of the Holy Spirit? Even though he couldn't have been any clearer that he was talking about sexual immorality and other blatant wickedness, I've decided that the Holy Spirit would never want *smoke* in his temple (except for all the incense and burnt offerings and stuff). In short, I feel pretty safe swinging this verse at you because it's been done so many times before that the context no longer applies (sort of like Kleenex, Aspirin, and Roller-blades becoming public domain from over-use).

Signed,
Anonymous

5. I didn't actually buy, read, or even open your book; I just saw it mentioned in a blog, so I went over to Amazon and savaged it. In fact, I'm not even reading this, so I'll never know you're describing me with almost frightening precision.

Ted Kluck is the author of more than ten books, but less than twenty books. He has written books on the following topics (and a few others that didn't make the list): Mike Tyson, the emergent church, professional indoor football, international adoption, pro wrestling, and the end times. His work has been translated into Korean and Portuguese, and he has received the Michigan Notable Book Award (2008), and two *Christianity Today* Book of the Year Awards (2008, 2009).

Ted also writes screenplays, teaches college writing, plays semi-pro football and loves his family. He holds an MFA in creative nonfiction from Ashland University. **www.tedkluck.com**

Zach Bartels is the pastor of an old-school Baptist Church in Lansing, Michigan. He recently signed a two-book deal with Thomas Nelson publishers, the first of which (a suspense novel about demon possession, holy relics, and a televangelist with really white teeth) will be in stores in October of 2014. He has also written satires and religious thrillers, and is working on a non-fiction book about consumerism in the Church.

Zach enjoys film, fine cigars, stimulating conversation, gourmet coffee, and spending time with his wife and son. He holds an MDiv from Grand Rapids Theological Seminary.
www.zacharybartels.com

Endnotes

[1] Yes, we're shilling for our other products. When you're a real Business Mogul (as we are), this is what you do.

[2] This may or may not have ever happened.

[3] Admission: Zach and I do this, frequently. If you think that makes us gay, go ahead and stop reading now. Antiquing is awesome.

[4] http://www.desiringgod.org/resource-library/ask-pastor-john/is-it-a-sin-to-smoke-or-eat-junk-food

Note that Dr. Piper's main argument here is that we must not be enslaved to anything (I Cor 6:12), referencing the very addictive nature of some types of smoking. He also makes much of the undeniable and considerable negative health effects of addictive cigarette smoking, citing the existence of warning labels on the box and indicating that before these labels were around, smoking probably wasn't a sin.

Note that Dr. Piper does not bring his argument forward seven verses to I Cor 6:19, as if Paul's concern with the defiling of the body (the Temple of the Holy Spirit) in that text had to do with cholesterol and blood pressure, rather than sexual immorality. Our little book will not deal with the question of health risks involved in cigar smoking, other than to say that cigars do not involve active inhaling and, in moderation, one cannot definitively show them to be worse for one's health than any number of diet-related dangers (i.e., too much salt, too much Aspartame, too much alcohol, eating a Big Mac every other Thursday)—and yet, the Lord ate red meat, which if done in excess can take a heavy toll on a man's health and drank wine, which if done excessively can summarily ruin a man in almost every way. Unsuccessful were my feeble efforts (not being a medical man) to locate a single definitive study proving that occasional smoking / smoking in moderation is any more dangerous than having a steak once or twice a week. (And, in fact, I might add, a cigar can go very nicely with said steak).

[5] http://www.desiringgod.org/resource-library/biographies/j-gresham-machens-response-to-modernism#_ftn20
If that sounds like something to strive for, I recommend a little study on the difference between piety and pietism.

[6] http://www.challies.com/christian-living/is-smoking-sinful
Very much worth reading, although the meta is longer than the Pentateuch and contains twice as much fighting.

[7] My church at one point in the past added an anti-magician section to its bylaws (since removed).

[8] This is certainly not an exhaustive list. We could add co-ed swimming, listening to any secular music (or jazz in particular, as it was once associated with liquor and promiscuous sex in many people's minds), and a thousand other things.

[9] Though it is, we discovered, the kind of place where you can get a cup of coffee to go.

[10] Of course, we've also met some legit authors in smoke lounges, like Dr. Bob Bennet.

[11] Yes, we saw that episode of *The Brady Bunch*

[12] Michael Weston voice here.

[13] Yeah, we know it's gopher wood in the Bible.

[14] Or perhaps it wasn't dry and you just got overzealous with your cutter and chopped off the whole cap?

[15] Although this may be misleading, since the darker wrappers actually come from the top of the plant.

[16] From the canons of the Council of Bob Jones University, A.D. 1951.

[17] Watchbloggers, feel free to have some sort of field day with this sentence.

[18] Minus, of course, the Human Growth Hormone, rash of head injuries, unchecked greed, rampant drug issues, and off-the-field problems among players. Other than that, the NFL is wholesome family entertainment.

[19] Yes, we know that "stogie" properly refers to a specific size of cigar (one which Jordan would never put near his mouth), but throughout this book we will use the term in its more colloquial sense, as a synonym for "cigar."

[20] J.R.R. Tolkien, The Hobbit, (London, J.R.R. Tolkien: 1966; Christopher Tolkien, 1994, renewed), p. 69.

[21] Despite what Ted says, any and all "antiquing" we may have done together has been in search of one of these cutters or lighters. Or other fabulous stuff.

[22] Our thanks to Phil Johnson for his unparalleled archive www.spurgeon.org which organizes the unfolding controversy for all to experience. Like everything on the Spurgeon archive, the page devoted to "Spurgeon's love of fine cigars" (http://www.spurgeon.org /misc/cigars.htm) is tirelessly researched and abounds with primary sources quoted in their entirety. If you love Spurgeon, www.spurgeon.org is a website you should be frequenting.

[23] G. Holden Pike, *The Life and Work of Charles Haddon Spurgeon,* 5 vols. (London: Cassel, n.d.), 5:138.

[24] The *Daily Telegraph,* September 23, 1874.

[25] *Christian World*, September 25, 1874

[26] G. Holden Pike, op. cit.

[27] *Christian World*, September 25, 1874

[28] As of the publication of this book, you can find the full text of Hutchings' tract online at http://medicolegal.tripod.com/hutchings1874.htm

[29] That said, these are a pretty good, peppery little maduro and we love it when the band is around the foot like that, rather than up near the cap.

[30] William Williams, *Charles Haddon Spurgeon: Personal Reminiscences* (London: The Religious Tract Society, n.d.), 31-32.

Again, thanks to the Rev. Phil Johnson, via his Spurgeon website, for bringing this anecdote to our attention

[31] Stonehouse, *J. Gresham Machen: A Biographical Memoir*, 1987, p. 506.

[32] We've both got kids and mortgages and generally gravitate toward $10-$15 cigars unless there's a special occasion, like the release of Gut Check Press's *Christian Gentleman's Smoking Companion.*

More Books From

Nothing complements a fine cigar like a delicious meal. *Saucy Broad: A Culinary Manifesto of Hope* is both a cookbook and a book about food and its place in our culture, our families, and our lives.

Cigars and boxing have always gone together like peas and carrots (or maybe raw eggs and salmonella).

Now Ted Kluck's award-winning book *Facing Tyson* is available in audio form (read by the author). This raw, eye-opening look at fifteen men who dared to step into the ring with one of the most devastating hitters of all time will captivate you with its stories of failure, greed, perseverance, and redemption. (Instant MP3 download available at www.gutcheckpress.com/tyson)

Gut Check Press

The prophet Elijah came on the scene millennia before the advent of cigars, but you can still imagine him lighting up, can't you?

42 Months Dry: A Tale of Gods and Gunplay re-imagines this ancient epic as a gritty urban thriller, full of smoke, dust, car chases, and shoot-outs, exploring the incredible things God can do even through flawed and broken men.

www.gutcheckpress.com

Gut Check goes out on a limb and suggests that Evangelicals are taking their own super-specific End Times Scenarios way too seriously and treating them as if *they* were the Gospel. This satire shows one possible end result, which winds up roughly 20% nuttier than what we already see on religious TV.

Beauty and the Mark of the Beast is the ultimate End Times extravaganza, complete with helicopters, grenade launchers, and well-tuned melodrama.

The End is near. Seriously. It's only, like, 45,000 words.

Fig. A

The Tongue-in-Cheek Guide to Hipsterizing Your Christianity

So you're thinking of becoming emergent (or whatever they're calling it these days)? You need this book like Bono needs wraparound sunglasses.

In *Kinda Christianity: A Generous, Fair, Organic, Free-Range Guide to Authentic Realness*, Ted Kluck and Zach Bartels equip you to dance as a PoMo Christian in the dried up river bed that we call LIFE.

This ground-breaking little book covers the following topics (listed from most important to least):

- Fashion
- Personal Grooming
- Finding the Right Workspace
- Choosing an Emergent Vehicle
- Naming Your Church
- Achieving the Right Atmosphere
- Your Internet Space
- People You Like
- People You Don't Like
- Dealing With Critics
- Diet
- Places to Be Seen (and not seen)
- Hobbies
- Theology

JUSt HOW REFORMED DO YOU think YOU ARE?

From the guys who brought you *Kinda Christianity* comes a new satire.

And this time, the joke is on us.

In *Younger, Restlesser, Reformeder*, you will learn everything you need to know to be a smug, young, trendy New Calvinist!

From what to drive, eat, and read to Calvinist dating (read: courting) techniques, you will not find a more comprehensive field guide to this fascinating culture, in which quoting Puritans is an exercise in relevance and every sentence ends with "@challies."

> "Bartels and Kluck show us that if we are to have a truly broad foundation for the concept of Christian dogmatics, we must begin with a discussion of the general principles of knowledge. They point out that the absolutely self-conscious God is the source of all human knowledge. Also, I really just like the pictures."
> —CALVIN JOHNSON, wide receiver, Detroit Lions

> "Ted and Zach toss lightning bolts of laughter out of their pockets like they are shooting dice in a back alley."
> —@johncalvin

Made in the USA
Charleston, SC
05 October 2014